HOW THE BIBLE CAN HELP US UNDERSTAND

WELCOMING THE STRANGER

HOW THE BIBLE CAN HELP US UNDERSTAND

WELCOMING THE STRANGER

A Bible study for individuals or groups

DENISE COTTRELL-BOYCE

DARTON · LONGMAN + TODD

First published in 2021 by
Darton, Longman and Todd
1 Spencer Court
140 – 142 Wandsworth High Street
London SW18 4JJ

ISBN: 978-0-232-53423-8

A catalogue record for this book is available
from the British Library

Designed and produced by Judy Linard

Printed and bound in Great Britain by Bell & Bain, Glasgow

*For my mother Fleur Cottrell and my
grandmother Margaret Gallagher.
Two migrant women who made their home
in God's heart and warmly invited me in.*

CONTENTS

SERIES INTRODUCTION

The Bible is the collection of writings and prayers pulled together by people and prophets over a period spanning approximately fifteen centuries[1] to describe humanity's relationship with God. It has great value for the three monotheistic religions, Judaism, Christianity and Islam, but as the key text of Christianity it plays a particularly vital role in the lives of Christians. Originally communicated orally, the written words of the Bible reflect the history, culture and theological understanding of the times in which they were written. In some instances, this can lead to contradictions, confusion and disagreements about its meaning. Nonetheless, the search for answers and collective wisdom found in the Bible's pages continue to make it highly relevant for the world we live in today.

The Jerusalem Bible was first published in 1956 by French scholars at the École Biblique in Jerusalem, in response to Pope Pius XII's encyclical suggesting a translation from Greek and Hebrew texts. In 1966, Darton, Longman and Todd published an English version of the Jerusalem Bible, using the French text as the basis. This version was edited by Alexander Jones and included contributions from well-known Catholics such as J R R Tolkien, and has always been praised for its literary qualities. Nineteen years later the New Jerusalem Bible edited by Dom Henry Wansbrough was published. Translated directly from the Greek and Hebrew, it incorporated new scholarship, fresh study material and the experience of two decades of use in churches. In 2019, Darton, Longman and Todd published the Revised New Jerusalem Bible, also translated by Dom Henry. This significantly changed version comes complete with updated study notes and inclusive language. It is one of the earliest new translations of the Bible in the twenty first century and has already been widely praised.

To celebrate the launch of the Revised New Jerusalem Bible, Darton, Longman and Todd have commissioned this series of study guides to the Bible. Recognising how much the Bible can teach us today and using the RNJB as the translation for the text, each book will take an aspect of life and ask how the Bible can help us understand it better. Each book will be written by a Catholic who will bring their own perspective to the subject matter. The authors are drawn from lay and religious, people with theological training and those without. Where many Bible Study Guides are written by Bible experts, this series is taking a different approach. Each author has been commissioned to write from their unique lived experience, using their personal response to key Bible passages to throw a light on the topic under discussion, reinforcing the intent of the Revised New Jerusalem Bible to be a Bible for 'study and proclamation'.

HOW TO USE THESE STUDY GUIDES

The format of these study guides is very simple. There will be a brief introduction to the topic, followed by 5 or 6 chapters picking up a key theme, leading to a concluding chapter. Each book is short enough to read in one sitting so you may find benefit from reading it through once before you start using it for study, and then focussing on one chapter at a time. You may wish to take notes as you go, to help with your reflections. Each book is designed to be read either privately or as part of a small study group.

1. Read the chapter through to gain an understanding of the author's arguments. Have a think about what they are saying, do you agree, do you disagree? Have you seen something in a different light?
2. Re-read again, focussing on the Bible passages referred to. Are the texts familiar to you? What do you think of the author's interpretation? Do you have an alternative one? Is this helpful to your life?
3. Each chapter is broken into sections with questions for you to reflect on. Use them as a springboard for further thought and your own independent study of the Bible.
4. The author's ideas and interpretations on the biblical texts cited are their own.

Readers may not agree with every position taken, but it is hoped that these guides will help provoke thought and deepen your own understanding of the issues.

5. Follow the recommended actions and review afterwards whether it has helped or hindered your understanding.

6. Use the final prayer and the Bible texts referred to in the chapter to pray about the issues highlighted.

7. If you are meeting as a group, consider the needs of those who might not be able to attend in person and offer the facility of Zoom/Skype, so they can participate virtually.

The study guides are produced in pairs with overlapping themes. This study guide is published as a companion to Bernadette Meaden's book on illness, disability and caring,[2] something that will be touched on later. Though each book has been written as a standalone reflection, some readers may find merit in studying both.

Virginia Moffatt
Series Editor

NOTES

1. *When was the Bible Written?*, International Bible Society Website: https://www.biblica.com/resources/bible-faqs/when-was-the-bible-written/

2. Bernadette Meaden, *How the Bible Can Help Us Understand Illness, Disability and Caring* (Darton, Longman and Todd, 2020).

INTRODUCTION

An open heart and an open purse have been the hallmarks of Christian life from its beginning.

An open door has always been a little more complicated.

I'm grateful for the opportunity, in writing this book, to explore the issue of migration and to think about the response that I, my church and my nation have made to those who seek a new life in our land.

Individuals, those in need, and the unthreatening stranger have rarely been turned away. But in any period of history where there has been a large influx of newcomers – Jews fleeing from persecution, Irish or Romany casual workers, or French Huguenots seeking asylum – the response has often been ambivalent. Vulnerable people fear losing homes, culture or livelihood. The instinct of those who live precarious and poverty-stricken lives is to cling onto the little they do have. The instinct of those whose lives are shielded from the harsh realities of the world is to keep the eyes averted. The challenge of the Gospel, however, is not ambivalent. Jesus tells us, 'whatever you do to the least of my little ones this you do to me' (Matthew 25:40). This is a challenge I believe we can meet together in our church communities through prayer and the inspiration of the Bible.

For the past 13 years, I've been volunteering at a drop-in centre for female asylum-seekers. During that time I've been privileged to meet refugee women of extraordinary courage and resilience. I've also been privileged to meet women who have given energy, initiative and love to their sisters in distress. These interfaces have taken place in church halls in the poorest areas of Liverpool, which has for many decades been a poor city. For me this has meant making journeys on public transport to areas of the city with which I was not familiar. So during this time I've not only become more aware of the realities of the migrant experience, but also to a lesser extent those of the host communities. While I witnessed a tremendous outpouring of love and support, particularly from churches, it would be wrong to pretend that tensions and legitimate grievances, on both sides, do not exist. Religious faith is a significant common denominator which helps forge understanding in these newly reconstituted communities – a fact often looked overlooked by those who think that atheism is neutral territory. I can't think of a better way for those of us who are Christian to explore the issues that need to be examined in this complex situation than from the perspective of holy scripture.

In chapter 1, 'How shall we sing the Lord's song in a foreign land?', I'll ask what it feels like to be an outsider either as a group or an individual. Using Psalms 137 and 142 I will look at the parallels between the Jewish people's experience of exile in Babylon and those exiled from their homes today by war and economic despair.

In chapter 2, 'Who is not my neighbour?', I want to look honestly at why the fear of strangers is such a visceral experience. I will examine the various ways this fear has been an aspect of self-preservation particularly in communities who feel most vulnerable. I will also examine how groups of all sizes – from families to nations – almost seem to need the concept, if not the actual presence, of an alien to create a sense of belonging.

Chapter 3, 'Fighting for the scraps from the table', takes an honest look at the competing needs of both the host community, who are already feeling dispossessed, and the asylum-seekers, who have come to live among them who are effectively disinherited. I will be looking at the competing prejudices and preconceptions both of those who champion migrants and those who are troubled by their presence. I will be asking what inspiration the Book of Ruth, the Sermon on the Mount and the Acts of the Apostles can offer.

Chapter 4, 'Everything in common?', looks at the commonality of experience shared by those who find themselves living in close proximity with people who seem so different to themselves. I will be exploring how all parties can work together for their mutual benefit.

In the final chapter, 'Old Men Dream

Dreams, Young Men See Visions' I will be looking at the generational differences in resistance to change and the sense of loss which can manifest itself as antipathy to migrants. I'll be examining how this can be mitigated by the values and virtues which migrants and asylum-seekers, bring to their new communities.

The terms asylum-seeker and migrant are used throughout the book. Sometimes I've used them together when I'm making general points about alienation prejudice and fear. In other places I use them separately because I'm describing particular aspects of different groups; for example I use migrant when I'm discussing the effects of economic migration and I use the term asylum-seeker when I'm describing issues such as the violence and menace from which asylum-seekers have fled. The term asylum-seeker has unfortunately become synonymous in some quarters with religious extremism, cultural segregation and illegal immigration. While some desperate migrants who can't find any legal means of entering this country do fabricate histories to give themselves a better chance of getting papers, it is a given that Christians are challenged to give help to anyone who needs it. We are of course also obliged to think responsibly about what form that help should take. Should we use finite financial resources to support economic migrants when those funds could be used to help those living in dangerous and degrading conditions in refugee camps? But as Britain is the fifth richest country in the world we might also want to ask why funds for the needy are so limited? A question that Bernadette Meaden also addresses in her book in the series, *How the Bible Can Help Us Understand Illness, Disability and Caring.*[1]

The books of Deuteronomy and Leviticus teach that strangers are to be welcomed protected and provided for. These books like most of the Old Testament were written after the period of the Jewish exile to Babylon. And I have referred repeatedly to this era to show how their national trauma informed Old Testament teaching on alienation and belonging.

In the New Testament Jesus sent his apostles out with the instruction that they were to depend entirely on the generosity and welcome of those who received them. His gospel was disseminated throughout the world by people who opened their doors and their hearts to strangers. The letter to the Hebrews exhorts us:

> Always to welcome strangers, for by doing this, some people have entertained angels without knowing it.
>
> *(Hebrews 13:2)*

NOTES

1. Bernadette Meaden, *How the Bible Can Help Us Understand Illness, Disability and Caring* (Darton Longman and Todd, 2020).

HOW SHALL WE SING THE LORD'S SONG IN A FOREIGN LAND?

1 REMEMBERING ZION

By the rivers of Babylon,
there we sat and wept,
remembering Zion;
on the poplars that grew there
we hung up our harps.

For it was there that they asked us;
our captors, for songs,
our oppressors, for joy.
'Sing to us,' they said,
one of Zion's songs.'

O how could we sing
the song of the Lord
on foreign soil?
If I forget you, Jerusalem,
let my right hand wither!

Psalm 137:1–5

The Southern Kingdom of Israel, a tiny state precariously positioned in the axis of three superpowers – Babylon, Assyria and Egypt – rebelled against its ally, Babylon in 590 BC. After a devastating siege, described in Lamentations, Zedekiah, the defeated king of Judah, was deported to Babylon together with his courtiers and the most powerful people of the land. The temple, the royal palaces and the walls of Jerusalem were razed to the ground. The Israelites were exiled in Babylon for 50 years. Those who had been used to comfort and control in their lives were faced with the struggle of finding a new way of making a living and retaining their identity. Like the asylum-seekers who currently find themselves exiled to Britain's (mostly northern) post-industrial cities (the highest number of asylum-seekers are found in Glasgow and Newcastle)[1] they found that they could no longer pursue their former occupations and lifestyle.

In 2 Kings 25:12 we are told that all the people of Judah were taken into exile except the rural poor – 'the vinedressers and tillers of the land'. This gives a misleading impression. Judah had a predominantly rural economy and the majority of the population would have been poor agricultural workers. Jeremiah 52 records that only 4,600 people were actually exiled.

The asylum-seekers who find a way to Europe also represent a tiny percentage of the displaced peoples of the world. Most of those who have lost their homes in the Syrian war for example are either internally displaced – fleeing from cities – or taking refuge over the nearest borders in Lebanon or Turkey. Only those who can afford to pay people traffickers and who also have the stamina to brave the dangers and difficulties of the journey have any chance of attempting to seek refuge in Europe.

The shocked and defeated Jews of the Exile had massive readjustments to make, just like the asylum-seekers living amongst us now. Many of them were also people of status in their home countries. For both groups, the adjustment to seeing themselves as poor, despised and helpless was enormous. Many of the Judeans found themselves doing manual, menial work which they had never expected to undertake and for which they must have been ill-prepared. Many would have found themselves cleaning their own homes and cooking their own food for the first time. And I know that this was the case for some of the women I met at the drop-in group. The Jews were however allowed to stay together as a community. This was a great blessing. The moral and spiritual support they gave each other created a cohesive group centred around a new understanding of themselves in relation to God and each other. This gave them the strength to flourish and prosper in their new lives. Many were so successful that their descendants chose to stay in Babylon, strong in the Jewish faith, but happy to remain members of Babylonian society when the exile was over. It appears to me that the women I know who have found it easiest to settle into their new lives have been those who belong to strong religious groups.

According to a recent report by the UNHCR United Nations refugee agency, the world is facing the highest levels of displacement on record. An unprecedented 70.8 million people around the world have been forced to flee their homes due to conflict and persecution – 30 million refugees, half of them under 18, are seeking a place to rest to feel safe and to make a new future.[2]

Some of them have found their way to Britain. People have been seeking refuge on British shores since time immemorial. The recent upsurge in numbers of asylum-seekers has had a major impact on many British towns and cities.[3] This impact has been most noticeable in the very communities that had the least cultural diversity – the towns and cities of post-industrial Britain. The lack of jobs and opportunities meant that these places were not attractive to economic migrants and had haemorrhaged their own young and hopeful. The resulting availability of large amounts of housing stock has been a godsend to a Home Office tasked with housing large numbers of new arrivals. So the inhabitants of these depressed areas – many with pre-existing social problems – became, without consultation, hosts to large numbers of foreign nationals with different languages, religions and cultures.[4] The refugees, too, had their own significant issues as a result of the traumas from which they had fled and the demands of the asylum process.[5]

> ' "If a foreigner lives among you in your land, you shall not molest them. You shall treat resident foreigners just like citizens, and love them as yourself – for you yourselves were once foreigners in Egypt."'
>
> *Leviticus 19:33–34*

Ideally, we would all show the generosity expressed here in Leviticus. In reality, our society can be hostile to migrants, particularly those who have exhausted the asylum process. So it is heartening to see how faith and voluntary groups often step in to help. Some years ago, I became involved with the charity MRANG, which was set up for ante-natal and post-natal asylum-seekers by the chaplain of the Liverpool Women's Hospital, Father Peter Morgan. He had started to meet increasing numbers of refugee women facing new motherhood who were alone and afraid. They lacked the emotional, practical and financial support they needed to face the challenges of caring for themselves and their babies. Every one of these mothers sang the lullabies that their own mothers had taught them 'on foreign soil', and they must have felt the sadness and loss expressed by the psalmist in the passage above.

My involvement with MRANG, began after I had spent a year living in Lille with my husband and six of our children in 2006–7. On the face of it, our experience of living in France was about as different as you could imagine from the experiences of refugees coming to live in Britain. When we arrived, we were, for the most part, welcomed with open arms wherever we went. People literally queued up to invite us to lunch each Sunday after Mass. Our teenage daughter was adopted by a charming group of girls whose parents were delighted that their children were doing so much extra-curricular English. Because we needed a large flat for our large family we lived in the smartest part of town and the children went to a 'nice' school. We were in Lille completely of our own volition. Home was easily accessible, and we saw our extended family frequently. We always knew that we could return to our normal lives at any time if things did not work out well. These were the optimum conditions to be 'strangers in a strange land' and yet it was still incredibly difficult.

Even with reasonable French to start off with, we would often miss verbal nuances and important information, sometimes with embarrassing outcomes like the time we turned up to a church council meeting with five children and a picnic. Ordinary tasks such as opening a bank account were immensely difficult and time-consuming and the delays led to cascading difficulties. The bureaucracy of the French education system meant that we had at least six forms to fill in for each of the four school-aged children, in French of course, and we felt a strangely intense anxiety about the agreement of our word endings because we didn't want to look stupid in front of the children's teachers. Nevertheless, we *did* feel stupid most of the time. We started laughing at ourselves and deprecating our national idiosyncrasies before anyone else could. We felt conspicuous and appraised all the time in a way we hadn't since our teenage years. The simplest of things seemed to be beyond us. It took two weeks to discover where we could buy a mop and bucket. The hall tiles were filthy, embarrassing under any circumstances but genuinely humiliating each time I answered the door, especially after my daughter had been given a cartoon sheet in her European Studies class showing national stereotypes. We discovered that British people are thought to be the dirtiest in Europe.

There were times if I had a bit of a cold, or I'd had a bad night's sleep, when I felt I just could not open the front door. I could not put on my 'French head' and spend a whole day trying to fit in. The most extreme example of this sense of alienation was when I suffered a miscarriage and felt so nervous about not being able to articulate my medical preferences clearly to a French gynaecologist that I genuinely feared I might be subjected to an accidental hysterectomy. So I stayed at home, pretending to the children that nothing was wrong (my husband was out of the country), instead of seeking medical help.

Because we always planned that our stay in

France would only be for one academic year, we knew exactly what the future held for us. But I found myself wondering constantly:

What it must be like for those people who knew that they could never go home?

What would it be like to be in a place where nobody wanted you?

Where you didn't really want to be?

Far from home, far from friends, far from familiar smells and tastes and songs and jokes and language that you could speak fluently, wittily and unapologetically. In a place where you never saw your own families' features and characteristics reflected anywhere. In a place where nobody knew your local history, place names, reputation and nobody cared that they didn't know. In a place where God (whatever you called Him), whose presence was invoked and acknowledged by everyone at all times, in speech and action, in every aspect of life, who governed every feast and fast of your life, seemed achingly absent. When you knew you couldn't go back home and you shouldn't go back home and yet your heart was longing to be there. That longing for home and the total disjunction between the old life and the new, which is such a shock, is expressed with elegiac pathos in Psalm 137 above.

I have spent hundreds of hours listening to the stories of the asylum-seekers who end up in our drop-in centres. They never expected to be 'asylum-seekers'. They never expected to be thrown into a world of poverty and dependency, of used clothes, used bed linen, second-hand shoes. They tell me about their inadequate housing, truncated education, language difficulties and the endless, endless waiting around with nothing to do and nowhere to go. This is the case when they have reached their destination. Before that many of their lives have exploded into a nightmare of fear, bereavement, mutilation, violation, and murky dealings with murky people. People-smugglers control the vulnerable. They force their 'clients' into an endless tissue of lies which will continue to trip them up and stifle their children's aspirations years into the future and create a constant sense of danger. And of course, for some there is always the very real threat of perishing on the journey.

Some years ago, I met a young woman at MRANG's drop-in who was clearly suffering from post-natal depression. She had a room in a hostel, three floors up from her cooking and laundry facilities. Despite having had a caesarean section, she had to walk up and down the three flights of stairs all day long while carrying her baby. I asked her what she did all day. I knew she didn't have a radio and no asylum-seekers in preliminary accommodation can have televisions because they have no TV licenses. She said, 'I look after my baby, and I read my Bible.' I was immensely moved that in her cold, depopulated existence – in the midst of pain and exhaustion – she knew where to find sustenance for her soul. She had realised that wherever she was, God was with her. She had only to call on Him. After that I often used to say to women of all religions, 'You are in a different place, God is not.' No soil is foreign to God. That young mother showed that we can indeed sing the Lord's song on foreign soil.

Questions for reflection
- What does home mean to you?
- If you have lived in another country, what did you miss most? If you haven't, can you imagine what it might be like and what you might miss?
- Do you ever wonder about the lives of migrants? What are the biggest challenges they face, do you think?

2 STRANGERS IN A STRANGE LAND

> With all my voice I cry to the Lord;
> with all my voice I entreat the Lord.
> I pour out my trouble before him;
> I tell him all my distress
> while my spirit faints within me.
> But you, O Lord, know my path.
>
> On the way where I shall walk,
> they have hidden a snare to entrap me.
> Look on my right hand and see:
> there is no one who pays me heed.

No escape remains open to me;
no one cares for my soul.

To you I cry, O Lord.
I have said, 'You are my refuge,
my portion in the land of the living.'
Listen, then, to my cry,
for I am brought down very low.

Rescue me from those who pursue me,
for they are stronger than I.

Psalm 142:1 – 7

The experience of being an asylum-seeker is not just that of losing country, family, and profession. It is also an experience of total bewilderment at finding oneself in this situation at all. This is not how asylum-seekers had ever imagined their lives would be. Psalm 137 is, at least, a collective cry of pain; but for many migrants one of the cruellest experiences is that of feeling utterly alone, of being a stranger in a strange land and cared for by no one. The desolation expressed pitifully in Psalm 142, 'No one pays me heed, no one cares for my soul', howls in the hearts of many migrants.

In her book, *Human Cargo*,[6] Caroline Moorehead collects the oral testaments of contemporary displaced peoples. She describes the experience of Tesfay, a 26-year-old teacher and political activist who fled from a small village in Eritrea. We can hear the same keening anguish of the Psalmist in his voice thousands of years later. Tesfay left home with only 24 hours' notice and without saying goodbye to anybody in his large extended family, except his father. People-smugglers accompanied him all the way from his village to a street corner in Finsbury Park, London, where he was left one freezing morning in January.

Because his flight had been so precipitate, Tesfay had not had time to prepare himself for London, to visualise what it might all look and see and sound like. He wandered the streets, fighting off his sense of panic, trying to understand what people were saying; he felt very cold and very lost. Sometimes, overwhelmed by memory and desolation, he fell over and lay under a car or along the pavement. Passers-by assumed he was drunk. The Home Office eventually granted him asylum and gave him a hotel room. The hotel was inhabited by sex-workers and drug dealers who he found terrifying and strange. The shared kitchen was very dirty so he stayed in his room and bought a kettle. He boiled pasta in it, switching the kettle on and off until it was cooked. He spent the days in his hotel room in his pyjamas going over what he had lost and the life he would have been living had he stayed at home.

'I felt everything as a shock, a pain, a loss. At home I had always felt safe. I was respected, popular. I had friends. I had money in my pockets. Here I knew no one.'[7]

For Tesfay and others, who have had to leave, home has become an elusive idea. Home was what defined them, and what they were forced to abandon. Home, in a place of exile, rarely exists. Tesfay says:

'Even if I go back to Eritrea now, I will not belong there. I will be strange to people, and they will be strange to me ... Wherever I am, for the rest of my life, I will never be entirely at home again.'[8]

> The Lord resolved to destroy
> the wall of daughter Zion,
> stretching out the line,
> not staying his hand from destruction,
> bringing grief on wall and rampart:
> they crumbled together.
>
> Her gates have sunk to the ground;
> he has broken and shattered their bars.
> Her king and her princes are among the
>   nations;
> there is no instruction
> and her prophets can find no vision
> from the Lord.

Silent, they sit on the ground,
the elders of daughter Zion,
dust on their heads
and girdled with sackcloth.
The girls of Jerusalem
bow their heads to the ground.

My eyes are spent with weeping,
my stomach churns,
my heart plummets
at the destruction of my young people,
as the children and babies
grow faint in the streets of the city.

They keep saying to their mothers,
'Where is bread and wine?'
as they faint like wounded men
in the streets of the city,
as their lives are poured out
on their mothers' breasts.

Lamentations 2:8–12

The texts above reflect the experiences of those who were taken into exile in Babylon after the fall of the Southern Kingdom of Israel in 590 BC. Like some of the people who come to Britain seeking asylum from war zones, the home they are remembering, for which they are so desperately homesick, no longer exists. The armies of Nebuchadnezzar besieged Jerusalem for three years then entered and destroyed the city. Society disintegrated in the face of fear and starvation. Everything familiar and good was gone. The people felt God had abandoned Israel. Memories like these are carried in the minds of some of those who seek refuge in our country.

The New Testament is uncompromising about the Christian response to strangers. They are included in the list of those who are most vulnerable in society and most in need of a loving kindness. In Matthew 25:34–46, Jesus seems to say that treatment of the vulnerable is a salvation deal-breaker.

'Then the King will say to those on his right hand, "Come, you that are blessed by my Father, inherit the kingdom prepared for you since the foundation of the world. For I was hungry and you gave me food, I was thirsty and you gave me drink, I was a stranger and you welcomed me, needing clothes and you clothed me, sick and you visited me, in prison and you came to see me." Then the righteous will say to him in reply, "Lord, when did we see you hungry and feed you, or thirsty and give you drink? When did we see you a stranger and welcome you, needing clothes and we clothed you? When did we see you sick or in prison and go to you?" And the King will answer, "Amen I say to you, in so far as you did this to one of the least of these brothers or sisters of mine, you did it to me." Then he will say to those on his left hand, "Go away from me, accursed, to the eternal fire prepared for the devil and his angels. For I was hungry and you did not give me food, I was thirsty and you did not give me anything to drink, I was a stranger and you did not welcome me, needing clothes and you never clothed me, sick and in prison and you did not visit me." Then they in their turn will ask, "Lord, when did we see you hungry or thirsty, a stranger or needing clothes, sick or in prison, and did not come to your aid?" Then he will answer, "*Amen* I say to you, in so far as you neglected to do this to one of the least of these, you neglected to do it to me." And they will go away to eternal punishment, and the righteous to eternal life.'

Matthew 25:34–46

Jesus' teaching seems simple and uncompromising. It applies both to welcoming strangers and caring for those who are sick and disabled, as discussed in Bernadette Meaden's title in this series.[9] However, our different experiences and perspectives give us different opinions about who is and isn't vulnerable, who is or isn't deserving of our common resources. We live in a society that habitually reduces complicated issues to binary choices. In its crudest terms our responses to migration, both personally and nationally, can boil down to 'Good high-minded people welcome and cherish all incomers without question. Racist bigots reject, vilify and persecute them.'

This isn't helpful nor is it an honest response to the gospel of love. The Sermon on the Mount invites us to think beyond our normal moral code to think the unthinkable and love the unlovable.

> 'You have heard how it was said, "You shall love your neighbour and hate your enemy". But I say this to you, love your enemies and pray for those who persecute you.'
>
> *Matthew 5:43–44*

Some of us find it easy to love and welcome migrants and the strangers in our midst. Some of us find it difficult to love and welcome migrants and strangers, for a variety of reasons pertaining to our own lived experiences.

Some of us find it difficult to love those people who feel threatened and diminished by migrants and strangers. Jesus' admonition to love our enemies, challenges all of us to open our minds and our hearts to each other. To move beyond our instinctive responses to a place where loving and including one group doesn't sanction us putting another group firmly on the outside.

In the next few chapters I want to look at the challenge to Christians of welcoming and supporting migrants while showing sensitivity to and understanding of the genuine challenges their presence creates for their host communities. It is important to remember that these host communities are usually the poorest and most dispossessed of our society. They are the communities that, until recently, the church has been most anxious to champion.

Questions for reflection

- Do you ever wonder what it must be like to be a stranger in a strange land?
- The Pope says if you don't follow Matthew 25:35–46 you can't consider yourself a Christian, but how easy is it to follow?
- Do you know refugees or migrants in your community or parish? What steps can you take to make them feel welcome?

TAKING IT FURTHER

In the summer of 2015, a series of stories about refugees crossing the Mediterranean hit the headlines. As the number of drownings rose, their plight was brought into sharp relief, by the picture of the body of three-year-old Syrian refugee Alan Kurdi, on a Turkish beach. Across Europe, many people responded with compassion, urging their governments to take action with the refrain 'Refugees Welcome'.

As a result, many countries welcomed Syrian refugees across their borders, with Germany being particularly generous.

Take a look at this YouTube film which shows the arrival of refugees in Cologne.

https://www.youtube.com/watch?v=z QJFfmxnuWc

- What must the migrants have felt as they arrived?
- How do you think their lives turned out afterwards?
- Why did Germany open its borders when countries such as Hungary erected fences?
- Did we in the UK do enough? Do we do enough?

PRAYER

Father of all
Be with those who have left all they know
Be with those who have lost all they love
Father of all
Be with those for whom the days are as long as night.
Be with those for whom the night is full of fear
Father of all
Be with those whose past is fading.
Be with those whose past won't go away.
Father of all
Be with the migrant and the stranger
And let them find their home in you.
Amen

CULTURE

Exit West by Mohsin Hamid is a novel of magic realism that tells the stories of refugees Nadia and Saeed who escape from their war torn city to Greece and then London via magic doors.

Refuge by Anne Booth, illustrated by Sam Usher. Refuge is a prose poem that retells the flight into Egypt from the perspective of the donkey. This beautiful picture book is ostensibly for children, but appeals to people of all ages with its powerful message of the journey to safety.

The Unforgotten Coat by Frank Cottrell-Boyce tells the story of two refugee boys from Mongolia who are living in Bootle, haunted by fears of home.

Human Cargo: A Journey Among Refugees by Caroline Moorehead is an investigation of the experiences of refugees around the world and the inhumane systems that prevent them from reaching their destinations.

The Optician of Lampedusa by Emma Jane Kirby is a true life account of an optician who witnessed the sinking of a refugee boat in the Mediterranean and was able to save the lives of some, but not others.

The Undercover Migrant (BBC podcast series *Crossing Continents*): Joel Gunter narrates the story of Azeteng, a young man from Ghana, who travelled undercover on the desert migrant trail north, exposing incidents of extortion, slavery and death.

NOTES

1. Migration Observatory Oxford, *Migration to the UK – Asylum-seekers and Resettled Refugees.*

2. UNHCR, *Annual Global Trends Report*, 19 June 2019.

3. Library Parliament, *CBP01403 – Annex – Dispersed and Resettled Asylum-seekers by Local Authority.*

4. Migration Observatory Oxford, *Migration to the UK – Asylum-seekers and Resettled Refugees.*

5. Mental Health Foundation, Mentalhealth. org.uk, *Mental Health Statistics, Refugees and Asylum-seekers*, https://www.mentalhealth.org.uk/ statistics/mental-health-statistics-refugees-and-asylum-seekers.

6. Caroline Moorehead, *Human Cargo: A Journey Among Refugees* (Chatto, 2005).

7. Ibid, pp. 232.

8. Ibid.

9. Bernadette Meaden, *How the Bible Can Help Us Understand: Illness, Disability and Caring* (Darton, Longman and Todd, 2020).

2

WHO IS NOT MY NEIGHBOUR?

1 STRANGERS IN THE COMMUNITY

Daniel, who was determined not to incur pollution by food and wine from the royal table, begged the master of the palace to spare him this defilement. God allowed Daniel to receive faithful love and sympathy from the master of the palace. But the master of the palace warned Daniel, 'I am afraid of my lord the king: he has assigned you food and drink, and if he sees you looking thinner in the face than the other boys of your age, my head will be in danger with the king because of you.' Then Daniel said to the guard whom the master of the palace had assigned to Daniel, Hananiah, Mishael and Azariah, 'Please allow your servants a ten days' trial, during which we are given only vegetables to eat and water to drink. You can then compare our looks with those of the boys who eat the king's food; go by what you see and treat your servants accordingly.' He

> agreed to this proposal and put them on ten days' trial. When the ten days were over, they looked better and fatter than any of the boys who had eaten their allowance from the royal table.
>
> *Daniel 1:8–15*

The priests and prophets of the Exile refused to see the defeat of the Southern Kingdom as a sign of Babylonian strength. They saw it as a just and inevitable punishment inflicted on the people for their sins of apostasy and syncretism. This interpretation – while excoriatingly critical – gave them the possibility of hope. Jeremiah, Ezekiel and Isaiah audaciously told the exiles that their captors had not overpowered them through their own superior might, but were merely instruments of God's judgement. If the people turned back to God, they could still regain what they had lost. Turning back to their God meant turning away from the religion and lifestyle of their pagan masters. The more they resisted integrating with the Babylonians, the stronger their national religious identity became. They theologised even the smallest domestic details of their lives, thus developing a portmanteau religion based around liturgies of table not temple. A form of their religion emerged which could be carried with them wherever they went. The law books of the Pentateuch were a manual for self-preservation.

Their criss-crossing of regulations, exhortations and prohibitions formed a cage designed both to protect the race and faith of the Jewish people and to keep out those who they feared might destroy them.

The Book of Daniel provides attractive role models to inspire the newly purified people. The brightest and best young men of Israel had been taken to serve in the royal court, to the very heart of Babylonian wealth and power. Daniel and his companions resisted all temptation to abandon their law.

What lesser people considered an honour – eating at the King's table – the Jewish youths considered a defilement. In Chapter 3, Daniel's companions – Shadrach, Meschah and Abednego – refuse to worship a gold statue, even to save themselves being thrown into the fiery furnace, saying, 'We will not serve your god or worship the statue you have set up.'

By resisting Babylonians' religion and values, the Jews fostered in themselves a heightened sense of purity and exclusivity. Such attitudes are common during large-scale migration. Those who find themselves relocated in a cohort who speak the same language, worship the same God and sing the same songs can create a shield around themselves and their children, which they hope will protect them from those influences of the host country that they find distasteful or immoral. However, until the host nation becomes familiar with the new arrivals this exclusivity raises barriers to friendship and acceptance. Both sides view the others with suspicion and often misunderstanding. This suspicion can be exacerbated if it is accompanied by economic disparity. If the incomers are economically vulnerable, they are despised. If they become economically successful, they are resented.

In the second half of the twentieth century, indigenous Ugandans perceived the Indian section of their population as economic and social usurpers. In the winter of 1972, the Ugandan president Idi Amin expelled all those of Indian heritage from Uganda, with only 90 days' notice. This led to 27,000 people arriving in Britain en masse. The host communities, mostly living in poor areas, were reeling from the first major period of unemployment the country had experienced for 40 years. They had received almost no information about the newcomers, and they were given very little preparation or practical support. Like the exiles in Babylon, the newcomers formed close-knit communites, and maintained strong cultural identities.

Prejudice against Ugandan Asians was widespread. I grew up near Handsworth at this time and although I, and most people I knew, considered ourselves to be well-informed about the evils of slavery, the struggle for civil rights in America and the horror of the Third Reich, and although we would never have used racist language, we did think it was perfectly acceptable to mimic Indian accents, turn up our noses at the aromas of Indian cooking and snigger at the vividly coloured paintwork that distinguished Indian houses. Why was this? It might have been a residual lack of respect for Indian people harking back to the colonial era. But I think it was mostly because we didn't know any Indians and we didn't have a back story to attach to the new arrivals. So, there was a nervousness about them, which wasn't helped by the little we thought we did know. It wasn't reassuring for example when we heard that all Sikh men carry knives 'in their turbans'. In that clean-shaven era, meeting groups of bearded turban-wearing and supposedly knife-carrying men was daunting to us. They looked menacing and we hadn't before encountered migrants who spoke a language we couldn't understand. We felt outraged when we considered racial injustice in the abstract. But we still felt vulnerable when we encountered the unknown.

Fear is an unsophisticated emotion. We were not so different to the 'peasant of old' described so superciliously by George Eliot in *Silas Marner*:

> No one knew where wandering men had their homes or their origin; and how was a man to be explained unless you at least knew somebody who who knew his father and mother? To the peasants of olden times, the world outside their own direct experience was a region of vagueness and mystery ... And even a settler, if he came

from distant parts, hardly ever ceased to be viewed with the remnants of distrust … All cleverness in some art unfamiliar to villagers was in itself suspicious … In this way it came to pass that those linen weavers – immigrants from the town into the country – were, to the last, regarded as aliens by their rustic neighbours.[1]

There is a legend that during the Napoleonic wars, when Francophobia was sweeping through Britain, a monkey escaped from a private menagerie and ran into the centre of Hartlepool. The inhabitants, fearful of imminent invasion, and having seen neither a Frenchman nor a monkey before took no chances. Without waiting to see what sort of threat it posed, they hanged it. This mistake has defined Hartlepool for centuries. But although the fear of the monkey was irrational, fear of the French was not. Xenophobia has blighted the world throughout history. It has hewn great chasms between people who could have mutually enriched each other, torn families apart and driven millions of young men to their deaths. However, 'xenophobia' means not the hatred of strangers but the fear of them. The instinct to protect ourselves and those close to us, even at the expense of rejecting others, is hardwired. But in the Sermon on the Mount, Jesus exhorts us to overcome this instinct, to aim higher than mere self-preservation. The Sermon on the

Mount describes a new order where unity of heart and mind is not limited to any one race. This core text of Christian ethics can't be read often enough. It challenges us to be bigger, better, nobler and more loving than human imagination and primitive instincts can encompass.

> 'For if you love those who love you, what reward do you have? Do not even the tax collectors do as much? And if you save your greetings for your brothers and sisters, are you doing anything exceptional? Do not even the gentiles do as much?'
>
> *Matthew 5:46–48*

I couldn't help noticing, however, that here – at the very moment Jesus reveals to us the mind and heart of God – the examples he gives of those we should aspire to surpass are gentiles and tax collectors; that is, foreigners and those who collaborate with the enemy. There are various places in the New Testament where Jesus and his disciples exhibit the ambient exclusivism of the post-Exile Jewish mindset. The most shocking example is Jesus' response to the Syro-Phoenician woman:

> Now this woman was a gentile, by birth a Syro-Phoenician, and she begged him to drive the demon out of her daughter. And he said to her, 'The children should eat their fill first, because it is not fair to take the children's food and throw it to dogs.'
>
> *Mark 7:26–27*

Jesus does listen to the woman and does cure her daughter. In doing so he makes it clear that her faith and her recognition that his gospel is for everyone is more important to him than her race. This is a pivotal moment in the new order of things. But the fact that none of Jesus' listeners would have been surprised by his words, not even the woman herself, shows how central Jewish exclusivism was to their identity and survival. The history of Israel is a history of expulsion, homelessness, constant waves of invasion, two deportations and near annihilation. The experience of exile led many to believe that – like the Northern Kingdom – the remnant of Israel would be absorbed into the surrounding nations and their distinctive faith would be destroyed.

Lord, we have become the least of all
    nations,
we are put to shame today throughout
    the world because of our sins.

We now have no leader, no prophet,
    no prince,
no burnt offering, no sacrifice,
    no oblation, no incense,
no place where we can make offerings to
    you and win your mercy.
                                    Daniel 3:37–38

But in an extraordinary turn of events, the
conquerors of Judah were themselves conquered
by Cyrus the Great, and the people were
allowed to return to their own land. They were
even allowed to bring with them the treasures
that had been looted from the Temple. This
miraculous return strengthened their belief that
they could only survive if they maintained the
ritual purity and exclusivity they had clung
to during their exile. The returned exiles felt
they had become so morally different to those
who had remained in both the Northern and
Southern kingdoms that they would be defiled
if they rekindled their former relations with
them. They even rejected the Samaritans' offer
to help them rebuild the Temple (Ezra 4:2–3).
In fact, the Samaritans became the most reviled
outsiders of all because they had once been

insiders. Where are they in Jesus' new order of things? Well, *we* know where they are because for us the word Samaritan has become synonymous with goodness and kindness. But for Jesus' audience the words 'good' and 'Samaritan' were a deliberately shocking combination.

And now a lawyer stood up and, to test him, asked, 'Teacher, what must I do to inherit eternal life?' He said to him, 'What is written in the Law? What is your reading of it?' He replied, 'You shall love the Lord your God with all your heart, with all your soul, with all your strength, and with all your mind, and your neighbour as yourself.' Jesus said to him, 'You have answered right, do this and you shall live.'

But he was anxious to justify himself and said to Jesus, 'And who is my neighbour?' In answer Jesus said, 'A man was on his way down from Jerusalem to Jericho and fell into the hands of bandits; they stripped him, beat him and then made off, leaving him half dead. Now by chance a priest was travelling down the same road, but when he saw the man, he passed by on the other side. In the same way a Levite who came to the place saw him, and passed by on the other side. But a Samaritan traveller who came on him was moved with compassion

> when he saw him. He went up to him
> and bandaged his wounds, pouring oil
> and wine on them. He then lifted him
> onto his own mount and took him to an
> inn and looked after him. Next day, he
> took out two denarii and handed them
> to the innkeeper and said, "Look after
> him, and on my way back I will make
> good any extra expense." Which of these
> three, do you think, proved himself
> a neighbour to the man who fell into
> the bandits' hands?' He replied, 'The
> one who showed mercy towards him.'
> Jesus said to him, 'Go, and do the same
> yourself.'
>
> *Luke 10:25–37*

After a couple of months of living in Lille our
ten-year-old son started to experience distressing
levels of bullying. When I asked him who the
ringleader was, he named the only child in the
class who hadn't been born in France – a boy
who had been adopted in Vietnam. I suspected,
and his mother confirmed, that before the
arrival of an English child in his classroom
he had been the butt of teasing and prejudice
himself. The presence of someone who couldn't
put two words of French together made him feel
like part of the core group for the first time. But
he could only maintain that sense of belonging
by keeping my son on the outside; so he used

the same bullying tactics that had been inflicted on him.

Strangers and outsiders seem almost to be a requirement for creating community cohesion, even within groups as homogenous as the Israel of Christ's era. Within the chosen people there were still sub-groups – Saducees and Pharisees, Zealots and collaborators, and of course those insiders who would always be outsiders – lepers, prostitutes, and those who looked as if God had punished them, such as barren women, the blind, those with unclean spirits. Their presence made everyone else feel just that little bit more chosen.

So there we have the paradox: strangers make us afraid of the unknown. The unknown help us to know who we are.

Except …

… in the kingdom of Heaven. One piece of Good News that Jesus has for us is that we don't have to play that game anymore. There are no outsiders in the Kingdom of Heaven. In the Kingdom, no one has to be out for someone else to be in. And if anyone does slip out, the good Shepherd will go and fetch him back.

Questions for reflection

* How you think the Babylonians perceived Daniel and his friends?
* Do you ever look at other community groups and find yourself resenting them? If so, why?
* Why do immigrant communities stick together so closely?

TAKING IT FURTHER

Read the story of the Good Samaritan, but instead of using a Samaritan as the person who saves the victim, change the Samaritan to a member of any group whose values or actions you find repugnant.

- How does that parable feel when updated in this way?
- Why do we have such feelings towards groups that are different from us?
- What does it say about us as a society?
- How can we challenge such views in ourselves and others?

2 THE FEAR OF THE OTHER

> Then Joseph died, and all his brothers, and all that generation. But the Israelites were fruitful and prolific; they became so numerous and strong that the land was full of them.
>
> Then a new king arose in Egypt who did not know Joseph. He said to the people, 'Look, the Israelites are now more numerous and stronger than we are. Come, let us take precautions to stop them increasing, or, if war should break out, they might join the ranks of our enemies, fight against us and then escape from the land.' So they put taskmasters over the Israelites to

wear them down by forced labour, and they built the store-cities of Pithom and Rameses for Pharaoh. But the more they were oppressed, the more they increased and spread, until people came to fear the Israelites. So the Egyptians ruthlessly made them work, making their lives miserable with hard labour, in clay and bricks, and every sort of field-work. They were ruthless in making them work.

The king of Egypt said to the Hebrew midwives, one of whom was called Shiphrah and the other Puah, 'When you attend Hebrew women in childbirth, look for the two stones. If it is a boy, kill him; if a girl, let her live.' But the midwives were God-fearing women and did not do what the king of Egypt had said, but allowed the boys to live. The king of Egypt summoned the midwives and said to them, 'Why have you done this and allowed the boys to live?' The midwives said to Pharaoh, 'Hebrew women are not like Egyptian women, they are vigorous and give birth before the midwife gets to them.' So God was good to the midwives, and the people increased and became powerful; and since the midwives feared God, he gave them families of their own.

> Pharaoh then gave all his people this command: 'Throw into the river every boy born to the Hebrews, but let every girl live.'
>
> *Exodus 1:6–22*

The Book of Exodus describes the liberation of the Israelite people from their subjugation in Egypt. It is their origin story, constantly referred to throughout the Old Testament. Because it is so familiar and has so many dramatic set pieces, we sometimes miss the import of the opening chapter. After Joseph's brothers had moved to Egypt to escape the famine in Canaan, their numbers grew exponentially. Over the next 400 years they grew from a group of 70 to make up about 25 per cent of the population of Egypt.

Although Pharaoh is the undoubted villain of the piece, it is clear that his motivation stems from a very real fear that the Israelites might be a danger to his people. But that cycle of fear, oppression, resentment, and retaliation only served to increase suspicion and ill-will on both sides. If the Egyptians were alarmed at the rate at which the Israelite women were producing babies, then the midwives' claim, that Hebrew women were stronger and better at childbearing than Egyptian women, only increased that dread. The Egyptians were afraid of being outnumbered and overpowered. But what seemed like swagger on the part of the midwives, was actually a desperate attempt to save Hebrew babies and their own lives.

The fear that a significant minority might form a fifth column of aliens who have no loyalty to their own country and might very well betray her to her enemies is repeated throughout history. It is the reason why Catholics were feared and hated in Britain after the Reformation. It's one of the reasons the Irish were feared at various times in this country, and why currently some people feel suspicious of British Muslims.

When I started researching this book, I was thinking of migrants largely as incomers from outside Europe fleeing persecution or economic despair. I had forgotten that my own great-grandmother ran away to America when she was thirteen. Her determination to escape the predictable life of a rural woman gave her the courage to seek work in New York City. Here she eventually married a compatriot and began to raise a family. When they felt sufficiently affluent, they took the children – and their furniture! – back across the Atlantic to Edinburgh. This was still exotically metropolitan, but close enough to home to cut a dash. She was proud that her children became priests and teachers. Like many migrants my great-grandmother felt a strong emotional pull to her homeland which she passed on to her children in songs and stories. These tugged on the heartstrings of my grandmother who during the stirring years of Irish independence felt that she should be back 'home' in Ireland helping to nurture the minds of the first free generation and to carve out the new history of her liberated land with the handsome young patriot who lived near her family's townland. For their children, however, rural life in post-war Ireland was even less attractive than it had been at the turn of the century. There were so few employment opportunities that my uncle – a classics scholar – could only find work as an occasional taxi driver while my aunt – educated in a convent boarding school – worked as a clerk for a wage that barely covered her bus fare. As a result pretty much the whole of their generation left. It was almost inevitable that my mother would join her siblings in Handsworth, Birmingham in the 1950s. Handsworth is an area that has been welcoming – or at least accommodating – migrants since the mid-nineteenth century. I had also barely acknowledged that, although I was born and bred in Birmingham, I've never really thought of myself as English. My first identity would I suppose be Catholic, and then for the most part Irish. My mother, her siblings, most of the priests and parishioners at our church, and most of the pupils in my primary school were first generation Irish migrants. We probably all had Irish accents. By the time I went to my convent school on the other side of the city I would have looked and sounded English but I've only ever had a strong sense of British identity when I'm in another country – most particularly when I'm in Ireland!

Because we lived in our Irish Catholic cocoon, I had no sense that we were different. We would describe those outside our church as 'non-Catholic' – as though Anglicans, Methodists, Baptists, Pentecostalists, Unitarians, Spiritualists, Jehovah's Witnesses, Jews, agnostics, atheists and Wiccans were all together in one vague, insignificant and peripheral group. So it was a shock when I casually told a girl one day that she looked Irish and she almost spat that she hoped she didn't. She said she was insulted to be associated with the people who planted bombs in public places and murdered each other. I was astonished that she could be connecting me and mine with the IRA! There was such a total condemnation of them at home and in church that it had never occurred to me that terrorism could be the public face of my culture and faith. I felt her antipathy was unwarranted and excessive, but I couldn't think of a reply and I didn't know why I couldn't think of a reply. Perhaps I had been forced in that moment to notice those tiny uncomfortable perforations in my wall of outraged innocence. My friend Margaret telling me – with disgust – that her sister's mother-in-law had held a collection for NORAID at her sister's wedding reception, and the acquaintance of my mother who said, she was appalled by the violence in Belfast but not sorry the British were getting a taste of it at home. For most of my childhood, the fear of random IRA attacks was a normal part of British life. The IRA were campaigning against the British military

presence in Northern Ireland. They brought fear
and death to British mainland, planting bombs
in public places and killing military and civilians
indiscriminately in an effort to draw attention
to their political agenda. Most Irish people in
Britain were living peaceful and integrated lives.
They didn't want to be identified as outsiders or
the enemy within. The same thing is happening
today with Muslim communities, who are
looked at with suspicion as a result of terrorist
attacks by Islamic extremists. The majority
migrant population don't condone the violence
perpetrated in their name. They suffer the same
fear of terrorist outrage as any other member of
the public. Yet they are viewed as complicit by
many of those who live in genuine fear of the
next attack.

The story of Pharaoh addresses why we fear
strangers and what that fear does to us.

Was the Egyptian fear legitimate?

As far as we can tell the Hebrews had been
contented and happy in Egypt. Apart from
Joseph's pledge to bury Jacob in the tomb
of his fathers, there seems to have been little
yearning to return to the land of Canaan. In
400 years they hadn't shown any tendency to
make alliances with Egypt's enemies. Did the
Egyptians fear being outnumbered or being
superseded economically? The Book of Genesis
does tell us that Joseph gave his brothers the
best land in Egypt. Did the Egyptians feel they
would become second-class citizens in their own
land? That is certainly the flipside of many of

the Cinderella stories which abound in migrant culture. These stories simultaneously act as a magnet to those continuing in need back home as well as a source of resentment to those living in need in the host country. In the Bible, characters like Joseph, Daniel and Esther not only gain wealth and influence in their adopted homes, but also manage to bring down violent retribution on those who have belittled and exploited them. But these 'what goes around comes around' stories continue the cycle of pain suspicion and retribution, carrying on from generation to generation, on and on into infinity.

It is tempting to embrace enmity towards the oppressors as an act of solidarity with the vulnerable or oppressed. But then we become part of the cycle, part of the sin. On the cross Jesus offers to break that cycle with his own broken body. His broken body says, 'No. It stops here. I will take it all. Lay your terrible guilt and your vengeance on me'. Whatever the origin of the pain you suffer or the pain you inflict, Jesus says on the cross, 'Let it end here. Enough!'

PRAYER

Son of God, Good Shepherd, Lord Jesus

As you did not pick and choose those for
    whom you died,

Help us not to pick and choose those for
    whom we live.

Grant us, Oh lover of all souls, that we
    might see your soul in the eyes of all
    those we meet.

Help us not to mistake familiarity for virtue.
Help us not to demand virtue before we are
     prepared to care of those in need.
Good Shepherd,
Take away our fears of strangers,
And take away their fear of us,
So that we might recognise each other as
     members of your flock sharing the same
     needs and hopes as each other and
     trusting in your loving Providence.

Questions for reflection

- Can you understand the Egyptians' point of view?
- Who do we define as strangers in our community? How do we feel about people who are different?
- How honest are we about our negative feelings of fear/resentment?

CULTURE

In the novel **Silas Marner** by George Eliot, the central character is unjustly accused of a crime he didn't commit and is forced to flee his home. He moves to the village of Raveloe, where as an outsider he is feared by the community, until he adopts a baby left on his doorstep.

Waiting for the Barbarians is a powerful and witty poem by C. P. Cavafy, describing the citizens of an empire waiting for the barbarians that they have always feared. In the novel of the same name J. M. Coetzee, inspired by the poem, explores Cavafy's theme that 'the barbarians' are a 'kind of solution' for the empire to subjugate its people.

Glasgow Girls is a play by David Greig based on the real story of seven schoolgirls who rallied in support of fellow pupils who were asylum-seekers.

A Trick to Time is Kit de Waal's most recent novel. She describes the experiences of young Irish immigrants against the background of the Birmingham pub bombings.

NOTES

1. George Eliot, *Silas Marner* (William Blackwood and Sons, 1861).

3
FIGHTING FOR THE SCRAPS FROM THE TABLE

1 THE OUTSIDERS

In the days when the Judges were governing, a famine occurred in the country and a certain man from Bethlehem of Judah went – he, his wife and his two sons – to live in the Plains of Moab. The man was called Elimelech, his wife Naomi and his two sons Mahlon and Chilion; they were Ephrathites from Bethlehem of Judah. Reaching the Plains of Moab, they settled there. Elimelech, Naomi's husband, died, and she and her two sons were left. These married Moabite women: one was called Orpah and the other Ruth. They lived there for about ten years. Mahlon and Chilion then both died too, and Naomi was thus bereft of her two sons and her husband. She then decided to return from the Plains of Moab with her daughters-in-

law, having heard in the Plains of Moab
that the Lord had visited his people and
given them food. So, with her daughters-
in-law, she left the place where she was
living and they took the road back to
Judah.

Ruth 1:1–7

In 1929 Mario Bergoglio left Piedmont in Italy
and sailed to a new life in Argentina. The pull-
factor was better economic and educational
opportunities. A big push factor was the rise
of Mussolini's Fascist party. It must have been
heart-breaking, saying goodbye to people he
knew he would never see again. The journey
itself was daunting; two years earlier, a similar
ship carrying migrants to Argentina had sunk
with the loss of 314 people. Mario Bergoglio
was lucky; he arrived safely and made a good
life in Buenos Aires where he met and married
his wife Regina. Their son George went back
to Italy in 2013 when the World's Cardinals
elected him Pope.

Taking the name Francis for his papal name,
the Pope committed his ministry to the service
of the world's poor. In the same year as his
election he went to Lampedusa an island known
as 'the gateway of Europe'. Here many migrants
land in dangerously inadequate vessels to take
their first steps on European soil. It's also the
place where those whose dreams would never

be realised, have found their final resting place. Pope Francis preached eloquently about our collective responsibility for the displaced people of the world.

> 'Where is your brother?' Who is responsible for this blood? In Spanish literature we have a comedy of Lope de Vega which tells how the people of the town of Fuente Ovejuna kill their governor because he is a tyrant. They do it in such a way that no one knows who the actual killer is. So when the royal judge asks: 'Who killed the governor?', they all reply: 'Fuente Ovejuna, sir'. Everybody and nobody! Today too, the question has to be asked: Who is responsible for the blood of these brothers and sisters of ours? Nobody! That is our answer: It isn't me; I don't have anything to do with it; it must be someone else, but certainly not me. Yet God is asking each of us: 'Where is the blood of your brother which cries out to me?'[1]

This impassioned advocacy of vulnerable migrants struck a chord with people around the world. The Pope drew attention to a tragedy which had been occurring repeatedly since at least 1997 when ships full of people from Albania sunk in the Adriatic Sea. In 2016, 1.8 million people arrived in Europe, 24,000 of them in Lampedusa alone, all of them fleeing something that seemed infinitely worse than the dangers they could only imagine.[2] Even after that peak, great numbers continued to arrive. Many welcomed them warmly. The relatively poor community – particularly the church – gladly sharing what they had. But as the numbers increased and the migrants themselves seemed to have their sights set on something better, there would be some who felt troubled by the strangers arriving in their communities.

The Book of Ruth, nestling between The Book of Judges and the Books of Samuel, describes the migrant experience through the lives of two different women: Naomi and her daughter-in-law Ruth. For Naomi and her husband the migrant experience had been a positive one. Their sons had lived to manhood and they had clearly welcomed their foreign daughters-in-law into their home. Had either of them been blessed with children Naomi may well have ended her days in Moab and her descendants blended with the Moabite population. Instead, grief drove her back to her own people accompanied at first by both of her daughters-in-law. Ruth and Orpah, whom she could have expected to provide for her in her old age. The tender relationship between these three widows is illustrated by the sensitivity with which Naomi releases them from their obligations. This is matched by the loyalty of Ruth who saw in her mother-in-law a trusted friend and the last link to her dead husband. This loyalty superseded the ties of family, religion and race. And so the two of them went to Bethlehem. A familiar name to us. The town that we fondly think of as little and full of hopes and dreams, feels very unfamiliar when we enter it walking in Ruth's shoes, conspicuous in the glare of full sunlight.

The two of them went on until they came to Bethlehem. Their arrival set the whole town astir, and the women said, 'Can this be Naomi?' To this she replied, 'Do not call me Naomi, call me Mara, for Shaddai has made my lot bitter.

'I departed full,
    and the Lord has brought me home empty.
    Why, then, call me Naomi,
    since the Lord has pronounced against me
    and Shaddai has made me wretched?'

This was how Naomi came home with her daughter-in-law, Ruth the Moabite, on returning from the Plains of Moab. They arrived in Bethlehem at the beginning of the barley harvest.
                                        Ruth 1:19–22

We may feel uncomfortable looking out through Ruth's eyes, but who are we in this story? Unless we have direct experience of being newcomers or outsiders, we are probably the Israelites;

the close-knit long-established community, watching, appraising, judging, maybe even fearing the stranger. And in the case of Ruth a stranger about whom we have strongly negative pre-conceptions.

'No Ammonite or Moabite may be admitted to the assembly of the Lord; not even their descendants to the tenth generation may be admitted to the assembly of the Lord, and this is for all time; since they did not come to meet you with food and drink when you were on your way out of Egypt, and hired Balaam son of Beor from Pethor in Aram Naharaim to oppose you by cursing you.'

Deuteronomy 23:4–5

Appearing at first to be little more than a charming folktale with a fairy-tale ending, the book of Ruth is in fact surprisingly radical. It shows a reviled outsider being welcomed and regarded favourably by a rich benefactor – Boaz – who offers her both sustenance and protection. The protection that she's offered is an indication that despite the injunctions of the law not all outsiders could expect to be treated well least of all a lone Moabite woman.

Then Boaz said to Ruth, 'Listen to me, daughter. Do not glean in any other field. Do not go away from here. Stay close to my young women. Keep your eyes on whatever part of the field they are reaping and follow behind. I have forbidden my men to molest you. And if you are thirsty, go to the pitchers and drink what the young men have drawn.' Ruth fell on her face, prostrated herself and said, 'How have I won your favour, for you to notice me, though I am only a foreigner?' Boaz replied, 'I have been told all about the way you have behaved to your mother-in-law since your husband's death, and how you left your own father and mother and the land where you were born to come to a people of whom you previously knew nothing. May the Lord repay you for what you have done, and may you be richly rewarded by the Lord, the God of Israel, under whose wings you have come for refuge!' She said, 'My lord, may I always find favour in your sight! You have comforted and spoken to the heart of your servant, though I am not even the equal of one of your servant girls.'

Ruth 2:8–13

Despite this self-deprecation Ruth eventually offers herself in marriage to Boaz, at the behest of her mother-in-law, and they all live happily ever after. And in this case it really is ever after because Ruth was the mother of Obed and Obed was the father of Jesse and Jesse was the father of David the greatest and most beloved king of the Jews even to the present day. This is extraordinary, there is barely any other place in the whole of the Bible where Moabites are not described with vilification and abhorrence, and yet here Ruth the arch-outsider is warmly acknowledged as the mother of the nation!

As Christians, we would rather see ourselves as Naomi or Boaz, not one of the tongue-waggers, or covert-glancers. But which would we be, really?

It is a powerful part of our Christian identity that our faith was born in an act of state-sanctioned murder and nourished by rejection and persecution. Martyrdom is part of the charism and agency of Christ's Church. From the death of Stephen, our first martyr, to the 18-year-old seminarian Michael Nnadi – who was killed in the first week of 2020 by Boko Haram – we accept that persecution is a possibility for those who follow Christ. In fact, without it the tiny Jewish sect of 'the Way' would not have grown and flourished throughout the world.

And it is right that this understanding of who we are, should affect our response to those fleeing danger or despair. Caroline Moorhead describes the desperate, disparate people arriving on the shores of Lampedusa: the boy soldiers, dodging death as they fled from conflict zone to conflict zone, but defeated finally by the cruel sea and the venal people traffickers; the pregnant woman, hanging onto a rock for dear life until she was rescued after four hours; the dead girl clinging so tightly to her sole possession, a small handbag, that her fingers could not be prized loose from the handle; the young man who wouldn't take off his sodden trainers because in them was tied up the money that represented, not only his own single chance for a decent life but also the potential opportunities for those who had sold land, animals and even their homes, to fling him, like an anchor, out into the future. Our response to these desperate people should reflect the Catholic social teaching which informed many brave souls during Europe's time of incomprehensible evil.

The Israeli historian and diplomat Pinchas Lapide has said that between 700,000 and 860,000 Jewish lives were saved by the Catholic Church during the Third Reich, and of course many other Christians made great contributions. We are familiar with Maximilian Kolbe who offered sanctuary and eventually his life to save his Jewish neighbours. Few of us are aware that thanks to the courage and commitment of religious communities, individual families and the Vatican itself, nearly 80 per cent of the Jewish population of Rome was protected from the Nazis, including the Chief Rabbi Israel Zoller who was received into the Church in 1945.[3]

Whenever I've heard stories of individuals risking their own lives and those of their families to save others I am full of admiration for them. When I was younger, I assumed that I, too, would have hidden Anne Frank's family in my attic. But now I am a mother I feel a passionate need to protect my own children and I am genuinely not sure whether I have it in me to be heroic at their expense. Maybe I would have been one of those people who kept their head down and hoped to avoid engaging with the evil that surrounded us. I'm not proud of my moral frailty, but it does stop me from judging those individuals and communities who feel threatened by the incoming migrants in Lampedusa and the other communities in Europe to which they are dispersed. I cannot say for sure whether the concern I feel for the fate of asylum-seekers and migrants would be as uncomplicated if my well-being or my children's needs were compromised by their presence. In the next section, we'll discuss the tensions that can occur in communities between the host population and the incoming migrants.

Questions for reflection
- How do you think Boaz' community reacted to him welcoming Ruth? How would you react?
- How easy is it to practise 'refugees welcome' here?
- What challenges arise from supporting migrants? What stops us from helping?

2 'ASYLUM-SEEKERS STOLE MY HOUSE'

And all the believers were united and owned everything in common; they sold their goods and possessions and divided the proceeds to all according to what each one needed. Each day, with one heart, they went faithfully to the Temple but met in their houses for the breaking of bread; they ate their share of food with glad and generous hearts, praising God and approved by all the people. Day by day the Lord added to their number those who were being saved.

Acts 2:44–47

In the Beatitudes (Matthew 5), Jesus teaches that poverty, loneliness and suffering are not signs of God's displeasure, but opportunities to experience God's mercy and justice. These passages are comforting and empowering if we choose to embrace them for ourselves. Unfortunately, they have sometimes been flung out as scraps of spiritual sustenance in place of economic justice – a point which Bernadette Meaden explores in her study guide on illness, disability and caring.[4] We can be confident that Jesus did not mean the Kingdom of Heaven to be understood as exclusively metaphysical by the counter-cultural way his disciples organised themselves in the first era of the church, as described in the above reading from Acts.

But this is not easy to achieve, particularly for those who already have very little. Some people in Britain – especially those who live with multi-generational poverty in the post-industrial towns and cities of the North – feel abandoned. The gradual changes that created modern multicultural Britain have largely passed them by. They didn't welcome incomers because none came. No one wanted to come and in fact no one really wanted to stay if there was a better offer somewhere else. Those who did stay were the people trapped by lack of money, aspiration or educational success. Families, parishes and communities created and sustained wonderful relationships and support systems, but in the world of mass media (and now, social media) no one could pretend that there wasn't a rainbow and that they were living on the wrong side of it.

For some, the sudden arrival of large numbers of people with different languages, religions and cultural norms is causing anger and resentment. People living in depressed and deprived communities already feel that they are bottom of the heap. They already have the worst housing, the worst schools, the worst job opportunities, the worst health and the worst life expectancy. Now in response to our collective compassion for the victims of war and social unrest on the other side of the world, it is these people and not the more affluent liberals, who are being asked to share the already inadequate resources they have been allotted.[5, 6]

This anger – although it is ugly, visceral, occasionally violent and unjustly focused – is not incomprehensible. Indeed there are many examples of it in the Bible. Those troubling words of Jesus about how our faith can grow or fade ...

> 'Anyone who has, will be given more; anyone who has not, will be deprived even of what he has.'
>
> *Mark 4:25*

... can – when taken out of context – have a particular resonance for those who feel that they and their children are always drawing the short straw.

To some extent, these feelings are reflected in the groundswell of support for politicians who claim to reject the power and influence of the metrocentric cultural elite. As I mentioned in Chapter 2, it has been a challenging aspect of this work that in reading the stories of Joseph, Daniel and Esther we find hagiographic tales of outsiders who have fought off prejudice and danger by finding favour with the powerhouses of Babylon and Egypt and then using this influence to vanquish their enemies – the citizens of the host nations – often with a relish for violence and vengeance which is distasteful:

The king said to Queen Esther, 'In the citadel of Susa the Jews have killed five hundred men and also the ten sons of Haman. What must they have done in the other provinces of the kingdom? Tell me your request; I grant it to you. Tell me what else you would like; it is yours for the asking.' Esther replied, 'If it is the king's pleasure, let the Jews of Susa be allowed to enforce today's decree tomorrow as well. And let the ten sons of Haman be hanged on the gallows.' So the king gave the order; the edict was promulgated in Susa and the ten sons of Haman were hanged. Thus the Jews of Susa reassembled on the fourteenth day of the month of Adar and killed three hundred men in the city. But they took no plunder.

Esther 9:12–15

These 'camel in the tent' tales provide cold comfort for those who identify as 'the people of the land'.

In the Channel 4 documentary *Sixty Days on the Streets*, a ravaged woman – with no teeth, but the last vestiges of great beauty still remaining – showed the researcher her little cardboard kingdom and described her longing for her six children now apart from her. Her addiction to drugs had taken everything

from her, but her own explanation for her
homelessness was:

> 'I haven't got a home anymore they gave
> my house to the asylum-seekers. Asylum-
> seekers have got my house.'

Of course she was making a scapegoat of an
easily identifiable target, but can we really ignore
her underlying belief that anyone and everyone
gets a better deal than she does? Are her words
offensive? Should she be silenced?

The poverty rights activist Darren McGarvey
deplores the way the voice of the poor host
communities is ignored by policy makers and
migrant charities. In his book *Poverty Safari*, he
challenges the idea that anyone with concerns
about immigration must be misinformed, racist
or stupid:

> The danger of dismissing concerns about
> immigration out of hand, or failing to
> appreciate the concern being expressed,
> is that people are excluded from the
> conversation about their own lives ... Yes, it's
> wrong that people should blame immigrants
> themselves, but it's not wrong to admit that
> immigration policy can have an immensely
> challenging impact in socially deprived
> communities ... where psychosocial stress
> is already endemic. We cannot decide to
> ignore social concerns or problems purely on
> whether or not we feel personally offended.[7]

In Chapter 1, I described the migrant community into which I was born. A constant stream of my people have been coming to Britain for many centuries. But they made their biggest impact in the middle of the nineteenth century. Between 1845 and 1849 hundreds of thousands of starving people flooded into Liverpool from Ireland, trying to escape the Great Hunger. The presence of these migrants devastated the city. On 23 of January alone, 24,000 were given relief on the streets. They brought deadly epidemics, criminality, prostitution and aggressive begging to what was then a small Lancashire port. They were a blight on the city and nothing could deter them. Such was their level of destitution that prison was 'as a paradise' to the half-naked, half-starved homeless families in the bitter winter of 1846.[8]And yet, inspired by the gospel, the churches and medical profession didn't hesitate to come to their aid. They clothed the naked. They fed the hungry. They gave the sick as much relief as possible and priests went in and out of the fever-filled hovels assessing need and giving the last rites to the dying. They worked without respite till they dropped. They must have been repelled by the stench and the squalor, and disheartened by the moral degeneracy to which starvation had driven the wretched souls. But they had the Sermon on the Mount engraved on their hearts and it never occurred to them to stop giving until they had no more left to give. Their efforts, particularly the attention they gave to the needs of children, providing immediate relief for hunger and shelter, but also establishing places of education and training, turned this catastrophe into the basis of a great creative city. As I write, the professors of English in Oxford and Cambridge are both products of a school that was started by the heroic Father Nugent for the sons of the reviled Irish migrants.

The newest incomers to these shores are often treated with hostility and suspicion in some sections of the media. When the right-wing press launches an attack on migrants and asylum-seekers however, they are at least giving 'benefit scroungers' a day off from ritual humiliation. I am not a right-wing journalist, but for many years I felt perfectly comfortable sniggering at the poorest people in society. I – and many of my generation – felt morally superior to our parents because we would not tolerate racist and sexist humour anymore. Somehow, though, we felt no embarrassment about laughing at Wayne and Waynetta Slob or Paul and Pauline Calf sketches. Somehow we failed to ask ourselves why all the unacceptable Irish jokes were more than palatable to us if we substituted the words '*Sun* Reader' for Irish. The social disorientation that the ridiculing and demonising of the poor can cause is described by Michael Merrick in his BBC talk, *4Thought-Socially Mobile?* Listening to his painfully lucid description of the binary choices he felt obliged to make as a clever boy from a working-class family, and the emotional pain these caused for him and his family, stopped me in my tracks because I knew I was complicit.

I've spent too much of my life criticising, attacking and objectifying when I could have spent more time supporting, nurturing and, above all, listening.

The gospel of justice and peace demands that we seek justice and peace for all. Some are struggling with the physical emotional and practical challenges of daily life that Bernadette Meaden describes in her book *How the Bible Can Help Us Understand Illness, Disability and Caring.*[9] Some have felt themselves to be at the peripheries of mainstream society for generations, hanging onto a decent life by their fingertips. Some have been catapulted into lives of distress by huge global forces beyond their control.

Must they be forced to fight each other for the scraps under the table?

Surely we can do better than this?

Surely we aspire to do more as individuals than to merely choose our favourite victim and then declare open season on their opponents. In his speech at Lampedusa, Pope Francis asked us to take personal responsibility for the inequity of our world. If we think things should change we must be prepared to change ourselves. Change will take effort on all our parts. We need discernment for justice to be established and discipline for peace to endure.

PRAYER

Holy Spirit, send the power of your divine
    love into the hearts of those whose lives
    are blighted by poverty, resentment
    or despair.

Repair the hopes of those who have
    forgotten how to dream.

Heal the hearts of those whose dreams have
    faded, or become the terrors of the
    night.

Let generosity prevail over self-interest.

Let understanding prevail over mistrust.

Let your churches grow and flourish.

                                                    Amen

Questions for reflection

- Do you think people in deprived communities have a right to express concern about immigration?
- Do those of us who are better off have a right to judge if we aren't faced with the same issues?
- How do we help such communities without endorsing racism?

TAKING IT FURTHER

Read the following article:

Community Based Approaches to Inclusion of Migrants and Refugees in Bulgaria. file:///C:/Users/virgi/Downloads/CommunityBasedApproachestoInclusionofMigrantsandRefugeesinBulgaria.pdf

Does it help you understand negative

attitudes to refugees? Do you feel any of the ideas would work in Britain? How can we enable our communities to mirror the early Christians?

CULTURE

Cecil Woodham Smith, *The Great Hunger* (Penguin, 1962).

John Furnival, ***Children of the Second Spring – Father James Nugent and the Work of Childcare in Liverpool*** (Gracewing, 2005).

Fuocammare, an Oscar nominated documentary by Gianfranco Rosi (2016).

Mrs Gaskell, ***Ruth*** (1853), a classic novel telling the story of a moral outsider and the transformative power of the Gospel.

NOTES

1. Pope Francis, sermon at Lampedusa, 8 July 2013 https://www.vatican.va/content/francesco/en/homilies/2013/documents/papa-francesco_20130708_omelia-lampedusa.html.
2. Missing Migrants website, https://missingmigrants.iom.int/
3. Pinchas Lapide, *Three Popes and the Jews* (New York, Hawthorne Press, 1967).
4. Bernadette Meaden, *How the Bible Can Help Us Understand Illness, Disability and Caring* (Darton, Longman and Todd, 2020).
5. Veenagh Raleigh, 'What is happening to life

expectation in the UK?', Kings Fund, 22 October 2019.

6.   Simon Duffy, 'Tilting at Windmills, or Radical Hope?' *Centre for Welfare Reform*, 27 March 2017.

7.   Darren McGarvey, *Poverty Safari* (Luath Press, 2017), p. 170.

8.   Cecil Woodham Smith, *The Great Hunger* (Penguin, 1962).

9.   Bernadette Meaden, *How the Bible Can Help Us Understand Illness, Disability and Caring* (Darton, Longman and Todd, 2020).

4

EVERYTHING IN COMMON

1 LIVING WITHOUT AUTONOMY

> Satan answered the Lord, 'But Job is not
> God-fearing for nothing, is he? Have you
> not put a wall round him and his house
> and all his domain? You have blessed all
> he undertakes, and his flocks throng the
> countryside. But stretch out your hand
> and lay a finger on his possessions: then
> he will curse you to your face.' Then
> the Lord said to Satan, 'Very well, all
> he has is in your power. But keep your
> hands off his person.' So Satan left the
> presence of the Lord.
>
> *Job 1:9–19*

The Book of Job is an unflinching exploration
of the experience of random suffering. Job is the
epitome of the 'righteous man' who is suddenly
tossed overboard into a sea of misfortunes.
There is nothing in his experience or philosophy
to make sense of what is happening to him. His
only recourse is to endure and to resist his wife's
temptation to 'curse God and die' (Job 2:9)

even though his faith brings him no comfort.

The Israelite religion was based, uniquely, on a moral code. Its rules were simple and its rewards and punishments played out in time and space. Job, and all who knew him, would have understood his prosperity to be the reward for his virtue.

> This man was the greatest of all the people of the East.
>
> *Job 1:3*

He and his 'comforters' had no concept of a metaphysical salvation, no sense – as Christians have – that suffering could be a morally enhancing or tempering experience. So Job suffered not only the loss of family, possessions and status but also the loss of his whole understanding of the world. His universe had become unfathomable to him and he did not know how to navigate it. He no longer felt he had any control over his life.

Our society places a huge cachet on personal autonomy. The cult of the individual means that everything from single-portion microwave meals to end-of-life decisions is perceived as an opportunity to express personal agency. We are growing increasingly intolerant of the very idea that there should be limits to any area of personal choice. In reality the lives of asylum-seekers and their neighbours living in poverty – who often assume they have little in common

– are united by their lack of agency and their similar approaches to negotiating with those who have so much power over their lives.

For migrants, this loss of control over their lives can be a sudden and devastating experience. From the moment they put themselves into the hands of people-smugglers, or worse, traffickers posing as international employment agents, they are obliged to disengage themselves from the people they once were and the universe they once inhabited. Like Job, many of them have been people of substance, professionals or those with elevated social standing. Their names, ranks or finances have opened doors, cushioned blows or mitigated outcomes throughout their lives. Relinquishing themselves to the control of others is seen as a transitory phase which will cease as soon as they start their new life with new papers and status. The reality is a huge shock. The average asylum claim can take years. Two-thirds don't succeed on the first attempt, so they have to wait for an extended period to negotiate the appeal process. During this time, they will be subject to endless form-filling and interviews, often not conducted in their first language. They will live in poor quality initial accommodation, followed by marginally better 'assisted accommodation'. They will not be allowed to take any paid work and even when they get their papers, well-educated, experienced practitioners may find that their qualifications are not valid in this country so they end up retraining for 'low-skilled', low-paid work.[1]

It is very common for those who have entered the country illegally to have had their original papers destroyed and to be given a false story and even nationality which, they are told, will enhance their refugee status. They are powerless to resist the people-smugglers' instructions, both because they have no one else to advise them, and because they know their families back home will be vulnerable to reprisals if they are uncooperative .

In her book *Some Kids I Taught and What They Taught Me*, Kate Clanchy describes a conversation she had with a young Indian pupil about another pupil whose family have papers, but still seem to have secrets:

> 'Yes,' says Amina, 'but that doesn't mean they aren't hiding something ... All refugees are hiding something.'
>
> I say ... 'They have to tell exactly the right story to get in. It's really hard.'
>
> Amina is nodding at me. 'And then they have to stick to it for ever! And they make mistakes, and they don't speak English ... All the people who actually get here, they started with money! ... They gave it all to people smugglers ... They take your money, and tell you to lie, because then they have a hold on you.'
>
> Her parents, in ignorance and fear, had to put themselves in the hands of people smugglers, brutal ones, who kept her father at sweated labour for years.

'Why do you think I'm not at university?'
asks Amina. 'Do you think, if I had clean
papers, I wouldn't be there in a second?'[2]

Whatever the pull factor of life in Britain – and
there are obviously alternatives to travelling
across many borders to get here – it is unlikely
that those who set their sights on settling here
imagine themselves in the conditions of poverty
and vulnerability that is the lot of those living
in the poorest parts of northern Britain in the
twenty-first century. The people with whom
they find themselves living are often frustrated
by a similar lack of agency but often without
the hope or aspiration of migrants. They have
a choice between doing the jobs nobody else
wants to do or not having any work at all.
Many families in post-industrial Britain have
seen their labour replaced by mechanisation
or by globalised industry chasing slave labour
overseas. Most recently robot-based retailing
systems have cut a swathe through traditional
– predominantly female – blue-collar work.
There is a prevailing sense that random good
luck, in the shape of lottery tickets, scratch
cards or a not-too-painful injury which might
convert into an insurance pay-out are the only
things which could significantly improve their
financial well-being.[3] In other families, parents
juggle zero-hour contracts, afraid to turn down
any job no matter how family-unfriendly in
case they end up on the naughty step and not
getting any hours at all. The effects of this

work-life balance on diet, health and education continue the cycle of deprivation and lack of social mobility which has been a signature of these communities for many decades.[4] It is the world of Universal Credit, Personal Independence Payments and Employment Support Allowance which Bernadette Meaden explores in her book in this series.[5]

Asylum-seekers and poor people both subscribe to conspiracy theories about being short-changed by the health system. They feel they are being given weaker or less medicine than they are entitled to because the system is prejudiced against them. A friend of mine would park herself and her children in her doctor's surgery and say, 'None of us is moving till you give me antibiotics.' One of our service-users told me she 'knows' that asylum-seekers are given poor quality medicine because her two-year-old didn't respond to the eczema lotion her doctor had given her but did respond to her friend's steroids! Both groups undoubtedly do suffer from worse health than the rest of society – not because they are being short-changed by the NHS, but because they have been short-changed by poor diet, high levels of anxiety, and insecure and unhealthy housing, which actually all create constant and costly demands on the health services.

There is tension between asylum-seekers and the host community over housing because neither has much control over where they live. Good social housing has been in short supply since the 1980s and failure to accept the offer of a property, no matter how unsuitable, will put an applicant so far down the waiting list that they are forced to seek, more expensive, private accommodation with inferior tenants' rights thus creating cascading tensions and insecurity. In the areas to which asylum-seekers have been dispersed, much of the available housing stock has been bought up cheaply by canny property investors.[6]

Asylum-seekers and benefit claimants make the perfect tenants for somebody wanting to make a quick buck. The rent is always paid and there isn't much pressure to keep properties well-maintained because those at the bottom of the heap have very little bargaining power. Asylum-seekers in particular like to keep their heads down and avoid confrontation because many don't really understand what may or may not prejudice their claims. The women I meet rarely make a fuss about damp, mould, vermin and faulty appliances because they fear it might bring them negative attention from the authorities.

Nearly 3,000 years ago, the prophet Amos decried the exploitation of the weakest and most vulnerable people in society. We still need to listen to his voice. We still need to listen to the voices of all who are calling for justice.

> Listen to this, you who crush the needy
>   and reduce the oppressed to nothing,
>   you who say, 'When will New Moon
>   be over so that we can sell our corn,
> and Sabbath, so that we can market our
>   wheat?
> Then we can make the bushel-measure
>   smaller
> and the shekel-weight bigger,
> fraudulently tampering with the scales.
> We can buy up the weak for silver
>   and the poor for a pair of sandals
>   and even get a price for the
>   sweepings of the wheat.
>   *Amos 8:4–6*

Questions for reflection

- Have you ever been in a situation where some aspect of your life was under someone else's control? What did that feel like?
- Do you have control over someone else's life? Can you relinquish it?
- How could refugees and poorer people in society have more control over their lives?

2 LIVING BELOW THE RADAR?

> There was a man descended from Levi who had taken a woman of Levi as his wife. She conceived and gave birth to a

son and, seeing what a fine child he was, she kept him hidden for three months. When she could hide him no longer she got a papyrus basket for him, coating it with bitumen and pitch, she put the child inside and laid it among the reeds at the edge of the river. His sister took up position at a distance to see what would happen to him. Now Pharaoh's daughter went down to bathe in the river, while her attendants walked beside the river. Among the reeds she noticed the basket, and she sent her maid to fetch it. She opened it and saw the child: the baby was crying. Feeling sorry for it, she said, 'This is one of the children of the Hebrews.' The child's sister then said to Pharaoh's daughter, 'Shall I go and get you a wet-nurse among the Hebrew women to nurse the child for you?' Pharaoh's daughter said to her, 'Yes,' and the girl went and called the child's mother. Pharaoh's daughter said to her 'take this child away and nurse him for me. I myself will pay you for doing so.' So the woman took the child away and nursed him. When the child grew up, she brought him to Pharaoh's daughter and he was to her as her son. She named him Moses, meaning 'Because I drew him out of the water'.

Exodus 2:1–10

This passage describes a desperate mother trying to protect her son from a harsh, incomprehensible law, a law which was designed to protect the Egyptians from being overwhelmed by the Israelites whose numbers were growing exponentially. While the rules and regulations of our welfare system are designed to be humane and supportive, they are not always experienced as such by those who feel excluded from the decision-making process by race or class. Both asylum-seekers and those who live on benefits or inadequate wages live on income levels which meet basic requirements but leave no wiggle room for the normal activities of British society, at school or elsewhere. They have no buffer for emergencies, wear and tear on household goods or unexpected travel costs. Tension levels are high when a family dreads something as normal as an invitation to a child's birthday party. Tension levels are high when you're trying to navigate a system which you feel is trying to trip you up all the time. Those living in poverty feel that their lives are operated by a big, faceless, hostile system often referred to as 'They'. 'They' give with one hand but obstruct with the other. 'They' operate within a bureaucracy which seems designed to be as inaccessible as possible. Forms are long and incomprehensible. Telephone contact is hard to access, eating up time with holding music and circular referencing. This causes more confusion, frustration and anger which has no outlet. There is simultaneously, resentment at being held at arm's-length, and fear that 'They' will get too near. This desire to stay below the radar comes from a general fear that 'They' might catch you out, might lead you to reveal something which will adversely affect your already precarious circumstances.

The possibility that their children might be taken into care is a prevalent fear for both communities. Anyone who has to seek help from social services – for example, needing childcare to cover the birth of a sibling – becomes subject to increased scrutiny and appraisal. Even those who fall outside of the categories we are looking at can feel vulnerable. I had a friend – a skilled tradesman – whose wife refused to seek medical assistance for her postnatal depression because they were both afraid that the baby would be taken away from them. These fears are not wholly without substance. Such is the cultural gap between service-users and service-providers that service-users often feel that they are subject to random penalties for offences which they and their peers do not perceive as offences. A common case is corporal punishment. This is a practice I feel very strongly opposed to and I welcomed the strengthening of the law prohibiting its use. Nevertheless, it is a method of disciplining children which has been in practice across the globe since time immemorial and cited as a moral obligation in the old Testament and other religious books.

> One who is sparing with the rod hates
>   the child,
> one who loves the child disciplines him.
> *Proverbs 13:24*

Some migrant communities who have different social and religious norms to British society would consider it bad parenting not to physically punish their children. They see themselves as the benign purveyors of essential character-forming, soul-saving chastisement. Many of those living in poverty also consider corporal punishment a part of normal parenting. However, schools are obliged to alert child-protection protocols if they see signs that a child has been physically punished. This can sometimes create an atmosphere of fear and mistrust between parents and the school system. The fear of sanctions and penalties for parents who feel that they are behaving appropriately may make them feel targeted and persecuted. This sense of outraged innocence is expressed by Job who is urged by his friends to repent for his sins so that he can be relieved of his suffering. He can't do this because he feels strongly he has done nothing wrong.

> Though I am righteous, his mouth may
>   condemn,
> Though I am innocent, he may
>   pronounce me perverse.
>
> *Job 9:20*

Lack of agency is the emotional wallpaper of both migrants and people living in poverty. The perceived – and actual – randomness of decision-making by those who have power means that the prevailing mode of thought for negotiating the system is not 'How do I conform to the laws of this land?', but rather, 'How do I make sure they don't find out?' My friend's father thought it was good parenting to cane his children. This wasn't particularly unusual. At that time, children were caned at primary school too. But he was a very strong man with tensions in his life which caused levels of anger that he struggled to master and he sometimes left marks which she and her siblings would cover up before going to school. They would have liked the excessive punishment to have stopped but not at any price. Like many of the families cared for by Social Services, they did not want any action taken against their dad. He was a good man who worked hard and wanted the best for them. He made them laugh. He took them on camping holidays where he did all the cooking. He meticulously marshalled the family's finances to give them advantages that he himself had never had. They didn't want to see him humiliated. They wouldn't have welcomed external involvement. They instinctively covered up for their own benefit as much as his. If they had seen school as an arm of the penal system, they would probably have disengaged themselves from school too. As it is they now have between them eleven degrees. And all of them have been contributing to society both economically and at community level for their whole adult lives. None of them feels disconnected from the state or its values. But neither do they feel disconnected from their father. They would be insulted if their dad were to be described as a child abuser, as would many of the children of those migrants who see corporal punishment as best practice. They didn't justify his violence towards them, but they did understand that he was informed by the culture in which he was raised. This clash of values and ideologies between different classes and ethnic groups needs to be handled with gentleness and respect on both sides. The prevailing belief that twenty-first-century British values represents the peak of human development isn't helpful. Many of the women I meet are shocked by the behaviour of British children and teenagers. They often perceive them as disobedient and disrespectful towards their parents. They consider them lazy at home and at school, contributing little but demanding much. They are appalled at their attitudes towards sex, alcohol and drug abuse. It would be very hard to convince them to adopt the parenting practices which they consider to have such poor outcomes.

As always what is required is an open conversation in which both sides can feel it is safe to express their ideas, voice their concerns, exchange good practice and find agreement on their common goals. Finding the right forum for this conversation is an urgent challenge. Lack of good communication leads to false perceptions which foster resentment on both sides.

In the run-up to the Brexit referendum I heard a lot of the anxieties and preconceptions of those living cheek-by-jowl with asylum-seekers. I listened to them making links between the lack of immigration control and their disillusionment with mainstream politics. Although my sympathies were with asylum-seekers, it did not seem irrational to me that people resented their own children being obliged to share limited educational resources with those who made additional demands on the system because they had little or no English, or had fallen behind in their education while pursuing asylum. However, at this time, my son-in-law was working as a supply teacher in primary schools across the city. His first-hand experience gave him more accurate insight. He noted that the children who made least progress were those in schools catering for white working-class children in extremely deprived areas. Their parents perhaps feel that many generations of compulsory education have done nothing to improve their own life chances so have little hope that schools will offer anything more to their children. They therefore have little motivation to support their children's academic activity.

In fact, for some, school is seen as yet another arm of the state. In schools with a relatively high intake of asylum-seekers the picture is very different. Many parents of migrant children are very aspirational, and highly motivated, demanding that their children behave with respect and industry at school. This can create a tipping point of peer behaviour encouraging all children in the class to raise their game.[7] Hopefully, this positive impact on schools in deprived areas, together with the children's own openness will create new bonds within the newly configured communities.

> During those days, as the number of disciples was increasing, the Hellenists made a complaint against the Hebrews, that in the daily distribution their widows were being overlooked. So the Twelve called a full meeting of the disciples and addressed them, 'It would not be right for us to neglect the word of God in order to wait at tables. You, brothers, must select from among yourselves seven men of good reputation, filled with the Spirit and wisdom, whom we should appoint to the take.'
>
> *Acts 6:1–3*

Even in the exemplary early days of the Church, there was tension among those who felt overlooked. But with good will and good communication, the problems were resolved. A few years ago I went to Calais with my sister to spend the money raised by her migrant support group. We were given directions about what to buy and how to present it. Most surprisingly we were asked to remove all the labels from the gloves, hats and even underwear so that they didn't look new. We were told this prevented fighting and bickering amongst the migrants since no one wanted to make do with second-hand products when their neighbour had something brand-new. The resentment which some groups in society feel that they may be being disadvantaged by what is given to asylum-seekers is only another manifestation of that struggle for survival, which also exists among the asylum-seekers themselves. This may cast migrants and their hosts in a poor light, but that desire not to lose ground is natural in any vulnerable group. It is a sign to oneself that one hasn't given up the fight. When we feel sympathetic to a group we like to think of them as intrinsically virtuous – 'the deserving poor' not 'the feckless or grasping poor'; the kind-hearted, community-spirited asylum-seekers, not the ones who would start a stand-up fight over a newish pair of trainers. But these are not Christian thoughts. These thoughts allow us to align our actions to other people's virtues rather than their needs. The exact opposite in fact of what we are exhorted to do in the Sermon on the Mount. When I am assailed by unpalatable behaviour I always turn to my mother's refrain which has been so valuable to me throughout my life, 'There, but for the grace of God, go I'.

In her article, *The Fragility of Goodness: Brexit Viewed from the North-East*, Anna Rowlands describes 'a common good conversation' following a talk she gave about the effects of migration in a Sunderland pub:

> 'one in which we attempted to speak and listen with respect to the diversity of views and experiences in the room. Searching for a sense of our common humanity and shared interests but aware of the real differences which should not be ignored.'[8]

She describes participants expressing not just their sense of loss for a pre-migrant age but also an aspiration. An aspiration to live in a familiar community with common experiences, pleasures and respect. An aspiration for people to look out for each other. These are surely aspirations shared by migrants too. Both groups are aspiring to something they had once taken for granted and perhaps didn't value till it was lost. A community can be created by a common enemy but it can only be sustained by the common good. In the past, the common enemies have been things like fascism or the lack of sanitation. More recently they have been school closures, loss of public spaces and the destruction of the environment. The common enemy as I write is the virus COVID-19. But in the face of that common enemy goodwill and community spirit are flourishing. Notes offering help are slipped through letter boxes. Teenagers are shopping for their grandparents. In the first phase of the pandemic we stood outside our houses every Thursday night to applaud the NHS. Our hands are raw with washing to prevent us passing on the illness to others. Mask-wearing is an act of mutual concern. These common goals create opportunities for us to discover and appreciate each other's strengths, sense of humour, experiences, fears and hopes.

Everyone living in this country, whether indigenous or migrant, will benefit by living in harmony, but we can't pretend that this is simple or instinctive.

The Bible can give us inspiration, idealism and paradigms for a healthy and sincere response to the needs of all those who are affected most directly by the refugee crisis in our world. Surely the great anthem of hope for all the oppressed is Mary's exaltation:

> 'My soul proclaims the greatness of the
>   Lord
> and my spirit rejoices in God my Saviour;
> since he has looked with favour on the
>   lowliness of his servant.
> For see, from now on all generations
>   will call me blessed,

for the Almighty has done great things
    for me,
and holy is his name,
and his mercy is from generation to
    generation on those who fear him.
He has exerted the power of his arm,
    he has scattered the proud in the
thoughts of their heart.
He has taken down princes from thrones
    and raised up the lowly.

He has filled the hungry with good
    things,
and sent the rich away empty.
He has come to the help of Israel his
    servant,
in remembrance of his mercy,
according to the promise he made to
    our ancestors,
of his mercy to Abraham and his
    descendants for ever.'

Luke 1:46–55

Questions for reflection

- Can you imagine what it is like to 'live under the radar'?
- How can government services build the trust of refugee communities?
- What action could we take to support those with less in our communities?

PRAYER

Blessed Trinity, model of inexhaustible love,
mutual care and perfect understanding,
Help us to love our neighbours without
reservation.
Help us to give what we can unstintingly
and receive what we are offered with
respect and gratitude.
Help us to abandon our prejudices,
withhold our judgement and embrace the
opportunities that you give us to
grow closer to those sisters and
brothers who have arrived in our midst
without withdrawing ourselves from
those whom we have always cherished.
Let our hearts expand to encompass all
those you have sent us to love.

Amen

TAKING IT FURTHER

Most of us feel a certain amount of agency in our lives but we also learn which areas of society are going to make us feel out of place. We learn to avoid them. For migrants, and those with lives severely limited by their poverty, this puts a great deal of normal life into the no-go area.

Choose a situation in which you might feel uncomfortable, like going to 'wait for someone' in the foyer of a fancy hotel. Perhaps you could go into a betting shop and place a bet, if this isn't something you have ever done before.

- How did this make you feel?
- Did you complete the challenge or bail out?
- How would you feel if that weren't an option?
- Does this give you an insight into how it might feel to be an economic or racial outsider?

CULTURE

The Displaced Person: in this novella by Flannery O'Connor (1955) a farm owner, Mrs McGinty, hires a Polish refugee. But when he proves more industrious than other farm hands, resentment grows leading to tragedy.

Americanah, a novel by Chimamanda Ngozi Adichie, tells the story of lovers Ifemelu and Obinze, born in Nigeria, who both migrate. After an uncertain start, Ifemelu manages to forge a life in the US, but Obinze struggles in the UK when his visa runs out. This is a witty and moving novel that documents the lack of choice many immigrants face, and what it means to return home after a long absence.

Ungrateful Refugee by Dina Nayeri (Canongate, 2019). A memoir of the author's experience of being a refugee in the UK and US, what it took to be accepted, and the constant expectation of gratitude required.

Who really runs Britain? The private companies taking control of benefits, prisons, asylum, deportation, social care and the NHS by Alan White (Oneworld, 2017). An investigation of the extent of outsourcing in the public sector.

Breadline Britain: The rise of mass poverty. Joanna Mack and Stewart Lansley. The largest survey of poverty since the 1980's, it demonstrates how poverty is due to structural issues in society rather than individual fault.

Underground, a 2017 Danish film directed by Julie Hoj Tomsen, follows the life of Ali, a failed asylum-seeker in Denmark who lives an underground existence in Copenhagen.

Paddington: The Movie. When Paddington Bear's home in Peru is destroyed, he makes a dangerous journey to England, where he seeks the hospitality of the Brown family. Based on the popular novels of Michael Bond, this film version seeks to portray immigration in a positive light.

NOTES

1. Jennifer Hurstfield et al., *Employability Forum: Employing Refugees – Some organisations' experiences*, 2004, p. 8.
2. Kate Clanchy, *Some Kids I Taught and What They Taught Me* (Picador, 2019).
3. Dr Gerda Reith, Research on Social Impact of Gambling, glu.ac.uk.
4. Kate Bird, *The Intergenerational Transmission of Poverty: An Overview* (CPRC, 2007).

5.   Bernadette Meaden, *How the Bible Can Help Us Understand Illness, Disability and Caring* (Darton, Longman and Todd, 2020).

6.   Deborah Garvie, *Far From Home* (Shelter, 2001). https://england.shelter.org.uk/professional_resources/policy_and_research/policy_library/policy_library_folder/far_from_home

7.   Rachel Pells, 'Michael Gove, Immigrant Children Improve Results and Drive Up School Standards', *The Independent*, 18 March 2017. https://www.independent.co.uk/news/education/education-news/immigrant-children-improve-results-drive-up-school-standards-education-michael-gove-london-dubai-a7637206.html

8.   Anna Rowlands, *The Fragility of Goodness: Brexit Viewed from the North-East* (ABC Religion and Ethics, 29 June 2016. https://www.abc.net.au/religion/the-fragility-of-goodness-brexit-viewed-from-the-north-east/10096814

5

OLD MEN DREAM DREAMS, YOUNG MEN SEE VISIONS

1 THE CHALLENGE OF CHANGE

The word of the Lord came to me,
saying:

'Before I formed you in the womb I
    knew you;
before you were born I consecrated you;
I appointed you as prophet to the
    nations.'

Then I said, 'Ah, ah, Lord God – look,
I don't know how to speak: I am only a
boy!' But the Lord replied:

'Don't say, 'I am only a boy,'
for you shall go to all to whom I send
    you
and you will say whatever I command you,
Don't be afraid of them
for I am with you to rescue you, says the
    Lord.'

Then the Lord stretched out his hand
and touched my mouth, and the Lord
said to me:

'There! I have put my words into your
      mouth.
Look, today I have set you
over the nations and kingdoms,
to uproot and to knock down,
to destroy and to overthrow,
to build and to plant.'

Jeremiah 1:6–10

In Chapter 1, we looked at the loss and despair
experienced by the people of the Southern
Kingdom after the destruction of the Temple
and the exile into Babylon. It looked as if all
traces of Israel would gradually disappear from
the land.

The subsequent restoration of 43,000
Jewish people to their homeland with the booty
that was stolen from the Temple does seem truly
miraculous. The first aspiration of the restored
community under the leadership of the priestly
class was to rebuild the Temple as the focus of
sacrifice and orthodoxy in a state that was now
effectively a theocracy.

The return of the exiles, which would
have seemed so unlikely to a purely rational
observer, was never doubted by those whom
God had appointed to be his prophets.

These isolated voices spoke repeatedly of the religious, not the political, import of the Babylonian threat. They had a spiritual clarity of vision that meant they could see both the necessity of suffering and the certainty that God would restore what was lost at the time of His choosing. They could prophesy with confidence that after a long period of exile the time would come when the chastened, contrite nation would reclaim their Promised Land. It is significant that the leading prophet God chose to proclaim the destruction of the corrupted Southern Kingdom and herald the future emergence of a new purified community of faith was a young lad – Jeremiah.

We expect the young to be visionary.

> Your sons and daughters shall prophesy,
> your old people shall dream dreams
> and your young people see visions.
> *Joel 3:1*

Old dreamers look to the past. Young visionaries are eager for what is to come. Jeremiah was fearful of this responsibility, but his youth meant that he could inspire his people with a vision of a better future which he himself might inhabit. He had a youthful optimism that there would be building and planting in Jerusalem once more – an idea which seemed inconceivable in the midst of devastation. And his optimism was vindicated.

The first task of the returned exiles was to rebuild the Temple – the focus of their newly purified worship. For the young the foundations of the new Temple represented hope. These were the passionate zealots who saw themselves as heirs to Daniel and his friends. They had no nostalgia for the old Jerusalem or even the old Temple, tainted as it was by the memory of former apostasy and offences against the Mosaic law. As far as they were concerned, this was Year One and their eyes were firmly fixed on the future. But the older people could only look back and lament what was lost.

> When the builders had laid the foundations of the Temple of the Lord, the priests in their robes took up position with trumpets, and the Levites, the sons of Asaph, took up position with cymbals, to praise the Lord according to the ordinances of David king of Israel. They chanted praise and thanksgiving to the Lord because for Israel and for his people he is good, and his steadfast love endures for ever. Then all the people raised a mighty shout of praise to the Lord, since the foundations of the Temple of the Lord had now been laid. Many of the older priests, Levites and heads of families, who had seen the first Temple, wept very loudly when the foundations of this one were laid before their eyes,

but many others shouted aloud for joy,
so that the people could not distinguish
the noise of the joyful shouting from the
noise of the people's weeping; for the
people shouted so loudly that the noise
could be heard far away.

Ezra 3:10–13

There is often a generational difference in
our response to change. Older people can
feel alienated by the language and mores of
contemporary life. Each generation considers
itself modern and liberal until confronted
with a further shift in society's norms. Parents
who felt they had always been open minded
about their children's sexual orientation –
even feeling pleasantly conscious that unlike
their own parents they had created a home
in which coming out wouldn't be a big deal –
might still be stunned if their child announced
they were about to have transgender surgery.
Those who cheerfully cooked a special meat-
free portion of Christmas dinner for the veggie
child might well be crestfallen if none of their
newly-vegan offspring would eat the buttered
parsnips, stuffing, brandy butter, etc., and
were vociferously affronted by the presence of
a turkey on the dining table.

For many of us change can feel like loss.
Our law acknowledges the importance of
preserving places of historical or ecological

significance, but the landscapes where we go about our ordinary lives have an emotional significance that we often don't notice until they begin to alter. When my dad walked along Soho Road in 1970s Birmingham, he couldn't find any part of his childhood there. The butcher where his parents bought the Sunday roast, the newsagents where he had his first paper round, the grocers where he used to bring back the pop bottles to get a penny on the lid, all the old shopkeepers – everything had gone. He often didn't understand the language spoken on the street. Sari shops, Indian sweet shops and halal butchers had replaced those with which he was familiar. He felt bewildered and, in a strange way, bereaved. In those moments he failed to remember that he had chosen to move out of Handsworth because he had been privileged with a good education and was able to buy a house for his children in a nice residential area with gardens and parks nearby. He forgot that there had been a huge economic boom in the 1960s, which meant many of the people he grew up with had also set their sights on something better than their parents had been able to imagine. He forgot that like most people he had stopped using the small – slightly more expensive, slightly less convenient – shops on Soho Road in favour of the supermarkets that had appeared in the shopping centres of the late 1960s. These supermarkets put all small shopkeepers out of business except those who were prepared to work very long and antisocial hours with huge amounts of unpaid family help. This is the life described in Sathnam Sanghera's novel *Marriage Material*, the life seen by many migrants as the first step on the ladder.[1]

The old people who wept when they saw the dimensions of the new Temple had forgotten that – according to Jeremiah – the old Temple had degenerated into a house of idolatry and faithlessness. They'd forgotten that this was what had had brought God's punishment upon them in the first place.

My Dad's sense of loss was very real and very painful, but at the end of the day, the thing that he had worked so hard to leave behind was poverty. And the new culture that had appeared in the streets of his childhood was simply the new face of the poor.

Questions for reflection
- What do you most miss about the world you inhabited as a child?
- What do you most cherish about your current environment?
- What would you be prepared to relinquish to help asylum-seekers and migrants?

2. TURNING THE WORLD UPSIDE DOWN

> Some of them were convinced and joined Paul and Silas, and so did a great many Greek God-fearers, and also not a few of the leading women.
>
> The Jews, full of zeal, enlisted the help of some ruffians from the marketplace, formed a mob, and soon had the city in an uproar. Setting upon Jason's house, they sought to bring them before the assembly. Unable to find them, they dragged Jason and some of the brothers before the city authorities, shouting, 'The people who have been turning the whole world upside down have come here now, and Jason has welcomed them.'
>
> *Acts 17:4–7*

When St Paul went to the synagogues to preach the Gospel of Jesus, he knew that there would be those for whom his ideas were too radical, too different for them to accept. These were, by and large, the Jews of the diaspora for whom – as we saw in chapter two – strict adherence to the law, as interpreted by the priestly class was the essence of their Jewish identity. Their orthodoxy made them feel safe and happy and they saw Christianity as a challenge to that security. For all of us the walls and ceilings of our emotional safe houses are familiarity and predictability.

Paul persecuted the early church, even before he realised how radical the Gospel was. Both he and those he persecuted saw it as another variation of Judaism – a sect like the Essenes. After his conversion he was completely reborn and blessed with an openness to change, which he recognised as the work of the Holy Spirit. By the time of the Council of Jerusalem (Acts 15), he was already thinking far beyond the horizons of Israel and Judaism. He was open to God's call to carry the Word to whoever was prepared to listen, and to do whatever it took to be effective.

> So, though I was free of all, I enslaved myself to all so that I might win more of them. To the Jews I made myself as a Jew so that I might win the Jews; to those under the Law as one under the Law (though I am not under the Law) in order to win those under the Law; to those outside the Law as one outside the Law (though I am not outside the Law of God, but under the law of Christ) to win those outside the Law. To the weak I became weak to win the weak. To all people I became all things, so that by all means I might save some. Everything I do, I do for the sake of the gospel, that I may have some share in it.
>
> *1 Corinthians 9:19–23*

But sadly there were those who felt betrayed by what they saw as a rejection of his Jewish heritage.

> Then some men came down from Judaea and began to teach the brothers, 'Unless you have yourselves circumcised according to the custom of Moses you cannot be saved.'
>
> *Acts 15:1–2.*

There are those in Britain who have been labouring in the vineyard for many years trying to spread the Gospel. They often feel dispirited by their diminishing faith communities. Some are heartbroken to see their churches being turned into Hindu temples or Sikh Gurdwaras. Others feel that, while their traditional Christian values are at best an object of derision and at worst targets for downright hostility, the religions of incoming migrants – which often appear enviably vigorous and proudly proselytising – are accommodated with respect.

The presence of significant numbers of new citizens who are different in their language, customs and religion from mainstream society can seem threatening to the host nation if it appears to be an agent for change. This isn't necessarily a negative attitude, rather an acknowledgement that life is good and we are happy, that our society has positive values and hard-won rights which we cherish and wish to maintain. Change presents a challenge for those in stable, peaceful societies because it means letting go of the bluebird of happiness to take a chance on those two birds in the bush.

In the post-war migration era, those who felt most fearful of changes to British life came from the more conservative communities. Recently however liberal sections of our society have begun to feel a similar anxiety. Some of the social freedoms and benefits that have been won by liberal activists in the twentieth and twenty-first centuries have been challenged by religious groups from migrant communities who have a different history and philosophy. For instance, the long-running demonstration by mainly Muslim parents against lessons about homosexuality in Birmingham primary schools has caused huge distress and recrimination on all sides as each minority group seeks to be supported and respected.[2]

An equally difficult struggle exists between those who promote animal rights and those Jews and Muslims who adhere to strict dietary laws. Lancashire County Council has banned un-stunned Halal meat from school dinners. This in turn has prompted calls from Muslim students to ban school lunches. Abdul Qureshi – chief executive of the Lancashire council of Mosques – has described this action as 'undemocratic and hugely discriminating.'[3]

Some feminists struggle with the fact that it is becoming increasingly common for Muslim women and girls to wear the niqab even if they were not obliged to in their home country. Some feminists see this ultra-chaste clothing as an affront to the British values of self-expression and female equality. Conversely, those Muslim women who actively choose to wear the niqab say that this attitude stereotypes them as weak and submissive. They see themselves as bravely embracing their counter-cultural faith in a way that liberates them from sexual objectification.

The truth is that nothing ever stays the same. Age, climate, economics, ideology, love, loss and religion all change our landscapes both mentally and physically. Migration is a constant thread throughout both Testaments of the Bible and has been a constant aspect of our island nation.

Few of us have much control over the events that affect migration patterns at this moment in our history. But all of us can very powerfully affect the daily well-being of those around us. Even those of us who have genuine worries about the effect migration is having on our personal situations can acknowledge that no individual should be held responsible for this enormous international upheaval. Very often it is the Church with its creed of brotherly love and all-embracing welcome which is at the forefront of breaking down the barriers of fear and suspicion. And the church has been one of the beneficiaries of the treasures that newcomers bring with them. Christian communities often find their congregations are swelled by devout parishioners from other nations. Despite the fears of those who feel Christianity might be overshadowed by Islam, the presence of confident, prayerful Muslim teenagers in our schools with their constant invocation of God's will and God's blessing is a striking contrast to the secularism of our age. Because they definitely 'do God' they have put religion back on the agenda.

Even the more conservative value systems of some migrants described above can be comfortingly familiar to those who feel that the world is changing so fast they no longer feel they are part of it.

When my thirteen-year-old great-grand-mother wanted to join her brothers emigrating to America, she planned and executed a daring flight. Waiting until they had departed, she followed their cart for seventeen miles keeping enough distance not to be spotted, but staying close enough to be guided by the sound of the cartwheels in the pitch black night. Her determination and energy are qualities often found in migrant communities today. Strong-minded individuals who are prepared to face and overcome enormous obstacles can greatly enhance the communities they join. The small business-es that open up in migrant areas bring foot-fall and new life to dying neighbourhoods. The economic impact of entrepreneurial migrants can have a hugely positive effect on towns and cities which have been in steady decline for many decades. New food, music, film-making and writing all enter our society via the churches, schools and social centres of reconstituted neighbourhoods.

Even though life never stays the same, human ideals and aspirations are surprisingly consistent. Most of us want to live in harmony with each other. Few of us want to sacrifice our culture, traditions and faith in order to do so. As Christians, our understanding is that God is Trinity, simultaneously diverse and whole. This doctrine is extraordinarily difficult to articulate, but it expresses a profound truth – an ideal for all relationships – and we who are made in God's image and likeness can at least aspire to that ideal.

PRAYER

Most Holy Trinity, mysterious God,
Let the glory of your distinctiveness and the intimacy of your unity be a model for the new communities coming to being in our land. Let each part of these communities share their strengths and treasures. Let all parts of these communities recognise and provide for each other's needs. We pray to you – who live in an eternal present – to give us the grace we need so that we may live joyfully, neither looking back with regret nor forward with fear.

Amen

QUESTIONS FOR REFLECTION

- Do you always assume that your own cultural values are right?

- How can our laws protect the rights of all minorities even when they seem to be so directly opposed?
- How can we show respect for cultural practices that seem morally objectionable to us?

TAKING IT FURTHER

Imagine being forced to flee your home and the country of your birth, eventually arriving in a place that is completely unfamiliar to you. You can barely speak the language, the food is strange, the smells are different, behaviours you take for granted are frowned upon. Write down the challenges you would face, and what skills and characteristics you would need to overcome them. How easy would this be for a child, a teenager, a young adult, a middle-aged adult, an older adult? If you are studying as a group, come back together and share your thoughts.

CULTURE

The One Who Wrote Destiny, Nikesh Shukla (Atlantic Books, 2019). Moving and funny novel chronicling three generations of a Gujarati family living in Bradford, tackles the struggle of arriving as an immigrant and the challenge for younger generations to understand their parents' experiences.

The Good Immigrant essay collection edited by Nikesh Shukla (Unbound, 2016). Excellent essay collection by twenty-one immigrant writers documenting why migrants come, why they stay and what it means to be other in a country that doesn't really want you.

The Boy at the Back of the Class, Onjali Rauf (Orion, 2018), a children's book about the effect the arrival of a nine year-old Syrian refugee has on his classmates.

Marriage Material by Sathnam Sanghera, 2013 – memoir describing the economic struggles of a poor migrant family in Wolverhampton in the 1970s. But it also explores the way that those who feel excluded often embrace the exclusion and resent those who want to cross cultural barriers.

NOTES

1. Sathnam Sanghera, *Marriage Material* (Cornerstone, 2013).
2. Nasia Parveen, 'Birmingham school stops LGBT lessons after parents protest', *The Guardian* 4 March 2019.
3. Jane Dalton, 'Council becomes first to ban unstunned halal meat in a move branded "Islamophobic"', *The Independent*, 13 July 2018.

CONCLUSION

The hand of the Lord was on me; he carried me away by the spirit of the Lord and set me down in the middle of the valley, and it was full of bones. He made me walk all around among them. There were vast quantities of these bones on the floor of the valley and they were completely dry. He said to me, 'Son of man, can these bones live?' I answered, 'You know, Lord God.' He said to me, 'Prophesy over these bones. Say, "Dry bones, hear the word of the Lord. Thus says the Lord God to these bones: I am now going to put breath into you and you shall live. I shall put sinews on you, I shall make flesh grow on you, I shall cover you with skin and put breath in you and you shall live; and you will know that I am the Lord."' I prophesied as I had been ordered.

While I was prophesying, there was a noise, a clattering sound; it was the bones coming together, one bone to another. And as I looked, they were covered with sinews; flesh was growing on them and skin was covering them yet there was no breath in them. He said to me, 'Prophesy to the breath; prophesy, son of man. Say to the breath, "The Lord God says this: Come from the four winds, breath; breathe on these dead so that they come to life!"' I prophesied as he had ordered me and the breath entered them; they came to life and stood up on their feet, a great, immense army.

Then he said, 'Son of man, these bones are the whole House of Israel. They keep saying, "Our bones are dry, our hope has gone; we are completely finished." So, prophesy. Say to them, "Thus says the Lord God: I am now going to open your graves; I shall raise you from your graves, my people, and lead you back to the soil of Israel. And you will know that I am the Lord when I open your graves and raise you from your graves, my people, and put my spirit in you, and you shall live and I will resettle you on your own soil. Then you will know that I, the Lord, have spoken and done this."'

Ezekiel 37:1–14

The prophet Ezekiel's vision came at a time when he felt utterly despondent about the fate of his nation. He also felt that his prophetic work had been futile. He was an object of scorn. He felt unappreciated and unheard by the people to whom God had sent him. They showed no sign of repentance for their sins. He believed that they were both spiritually and politically past redemption. He could see no hope. And at the outset, his vision – a valley of dry bones – seemed to be a perfect illustration of his desolation. Judaism had no doctrine of the afterlife at this point. A desiccated body represented the end of everything. But at the beginning of Genesis, God's Word had brought forth life from nothing. When Ezekiel speaks God's word, his breath carries God's creative spirit into the lifeless landscape, wakes the dead, and changes despair into hope.

When we look at the world's displaced peoples, their needs, their distress and their disappointments, it is hard to be hopeful that a just and speedy resolution to their problems will be found. This is partly because the original causes of their displacement are so intractable, and partly because the problem is so complex that no one body is strong enough, or interested enough to address it. How can we feel optimistic? The message of Ezekiel reminds us to have faith that truly all things are possible with God. True hope is not passive. It girds the loins for action. In the preceding chapters, I've tried to address the anxieties of those most affected by migration. But the changes that have affected this country are dwarfed by the changes that have occurred in those areas of the world where the refugee crisis originated. War, climate change and sectarian violence have left millions facing a future they could never have imagined. David Nott is a surgeon who has volunteered in all the major war zones of the world over the last twenty years In his book *War Doctor*, he describes the fall of Aleppo – a once prosperous and modern city:

> Back in East Aleppo, the ruined streets were deserted. No one walked anywhere through choice anymore. It was simply too dangerous. We passed a school that had been bombed. It must've been at least four or five storeys high, but was now flattened. On the ground floor you could still see child-sized desks and chairs poking out from the rubble. The smell of death seemed more concentrated here than elsewhere. There must have been children in the building when the bomb fell. We were hurrying now, anxious to be home. Suddenly, the unearthly calm was shattered by the arrival of a Syrian fighter jet overhead. We were out in the open and the pilot had obviously seen us. He turned in a hard circle to come around again. The four of us froze. Amma began shouting for us to take cover, but there was nowhere to take cover apart from a wall some distance away. We ran towards it and crouched down as the plane came round once more waiting for the moment to strike ... The noise of

the engines became deafening, but even that was drowned out by the blast of the rockets hitting the buildings around us.[1]

Which of us would not want to get as far as possible from this violence? Which of us would not want to live in the prosperous peaceful country to which David's father came as a migrant in the 1950s?

I don't feel blasé about the changes that migration has brought to this country.

I feel anxious about community harmony.

I feel anxious about racism.

I feel anxious about the strain of ever-growing numbers on our health and social services.

Of course we need to find solutions to these problems.

But I am appalled when I look at the lives lived by those in refugee camps.

Those who have had to flee terrifying situations.

Those who have had to make choices about who to bring with them and who to abandon on the way.

Those whose children are not growing because they have insufficient food.

Those whose children are not getting anything like a decent education.

Those for whom each bleak day is followed by another bleak day.

Those who are infantilised by their inability to do anything for themselves or their dependents, and who are prepared to throw whatever they have at any desperate opportunity to get out.

In her book *Human Cargo*, Caroline Moorehead describes refugees in the camp on the border of Guinea. One of her most heart rending sentences is: 'most of them do not even have a bucket, And they think about one and talk about one with longing.'[2]

I am appalled when I look at my television and see nearly 4,000,000 people living in these desperate conditions in Turkish refugee camps to keep them out of Europe. As I write, all the governments of the world are gearing up to resist the COVID-19 pandemic. By the time you read this you will know how it has turned out, but how can it not bring even more anxiety and suffering to those in the refugee camps whose lives are already unbearable? Whatever happens the activity of this tiny virus is amplifying what St Paul teaches us in his first letter to the Corinthians:

> And indeed the body consists not of one member but of many. If the foot were to say, 'I am not a hand and so I do not belong to the body,' it does not belong to the body any the less for that. Or if the ear were to say, 'I am not an eye, and so I do not belong to the body,' it does not belong to the body any the less for that. If the whole body were an eye, where would hearing be? If the whole

> body were hearing, where would the sense of smell be? But as it is, God has put all the members into the body as he chose. If they were all the same member, where would the body be? As it is, the members are many but the body is one. The eye cannot say to the hand, 'I do not need you,' nor can the head say to the feet, 'I do not need you.'
>
> *1 Corinthians 12:14–24*

We are all interconnected and our actions affect each other. Christians have been speaking out for many years against the arms trade and against unfair commodity trading which have such devastating impact on the lives of people we never see. In 2009 Pope Benedict XVI – in his encyclical *Caritas in Veritae* – denounced the damage done to the poorest people in the world by rapacious global markets.[3]

For the most part, western society took little notice of how interdependent our lives were with those in Less Economically Developed Countries. We didn't ask where our incredibly cheap food and clothes came from, nor how the people who produced them survived. But the COVID-19 pandemic has forced us to look at how interconnected our lives really are.

How can people living with immune systems diminished by poor diet and high stress resist infection?

How can people living in an overcrowded refugee camp with inadequate sanitary conditions be able to wash their hands for 30 seconds and dry them on a clean towel every time they go to the toilet?

They can't.

Even if government treaties try to keep them in this twilight zone of penal protection, the growth industry of people-smuggling is so well established now that we have no way of monitoring whether those who cross our borders are infected or not. How many of us would sit around waiting to be infected if we had any means to get ourselves and our children out of a fever pit?

John Donne said no man is an island.

We had better wake up quickly to the fact that no island is an island anymore.

> No man is an island,
> Entire of itself,
> Every man is a piece of the continent,
> A part of the main.
> If a clod be washed away by the sea,
> Europe is the less.
> As well as if a promontory were.
> As well as if a manor of thy friend's
> Or of thine own were:
> Any man's death diminishes me,
> Because I am involved in mankind,
> And therefore never send to know for whom
>   the bell tolls;
> It tolls for thee.
>
> *John Donne*

I started writing this book feeling confident that I was well-informed about the issues of migration, asylum and resettlement. Not because I had any part in policy or its implementation, but because I'd spent so many hundreds of hours listening to women describing their asylum experience and accompanying them, where possible, when they have faced daunting situations. But of course the more I've researched the issues the more complex they have shown themselves to be. There are important areas I would like to have explored here, but I ran out of space – for instance, the impact of migration on the rise of the far right, particularly in Germany, which has been the most welcoming country in Europe. I haven't covered the dubious morality of asset-stripping skills and talents by encouraging migration from LED countries instead of spending money on training and education here at home.

Migration is also decimating the populations of poor Eastern European countries. In 2015, for example, 2.3 per cent of Albania's tiny population applied for asylum status in Germany alone.[4] The young and strong are leaving the old and weak to support each other. We need to ask ourselves whether our warm welcome for those we need to nurse and build and care in our own country is leaving a cold wind of loneliness and disintegration back in their homeland?

St Paul tells us in 1 Corinthians 13:13 that loving kindness is the greatest virtue, but even kindness itself is hard to define if we are going to be judicious about its effects. The roots of mass migration are entangled with those of so many other moral dilemmas that it seems futile to attempt to isolate them. I wasn't really expecting to come to any well-defined conclusion but in fact it does seem clear to me that the most fundamental factor – even for those fleeing wars which appear to be based on ideology – is greed and the resulting resentment it engenders. Unless we collectively acknowledge this root cause of so many of the world's problems there will be more conflict and disruption ahead. I am thinking in particular of the effects of over-consumption on the environment. This will have a future impact on migration patterns which few of us have contemplated. John Lanchester's book *The Wall*, which describes a dystopian Britain channelling much of its resources into repelling the desperate migrants determined to find refuge from the sea which has engulfed their homelands, may prove to be prophetic.[4]

What should our Christian response be?

If we take heed of the Saint Paul's Letter to Timothy (1 Tim 6:6-10), it should be a new blossoming of contentment.

Relishing what we do have instead of striving for what we don't.

Noticing our own blessings instead of envying those of others.

Savouring the present pleasure instead of rushing forward to the next novel experience.

Enjoying the fruits of our labour instead of labouring incessantly for a harvest that we have no time to enjoy.

This is not a gospel of self-denial and sacrifice. It is a gospel of enough!

Not just acknowledging that most of us have enough consumer goods, but also that we have had enough of striving, enough of pushing and shoving, enough of grabbing more than our fair share, enough of guarding it fearfully, enough of binging, enough of dieting, enough of broken resolutions, enough of waste disposal problems, enough pollution.

By embracing this spirit of contentment we simultaneously release others from the scourge of want and ourselves from the scourge of endlessly, insatiably, wanting.

While it sometimes appears that the mass consumerism of the past 50 years is hegemonic, green shoots of hope are everywhere. The ideology of individualism and excess self-gratification is being challenged by some of the next generation, but also by the prophetic leadership of Pope Francis in his encyclical *Laudato Si'*. I began this conclusion with Ezekiel's vision of hope because I do have tremendous hope, hope that is based equally on the wisdom of our Holy Father and the idealism of our children.

NOTES

1. David Nott, *War Doctor – Surgery on the Frontline* (Picador, 2019), p. 286.

2. Caroline Moorehead, *Human Cargo* (Penguin Books, 2005).
3. Pope Benedict XV1 encyclical, *Caritas in Veritae*, 29 June 2009.
4. Reuters, 'Albania migration trends change', 19 October 2018.
5. John Lanchester, *The Wall* (Faber, 2019).

ACKNOWLEDGEMENTS

I would like to thank Virginia Moffatt for inviting me to contribute to this series, and for her unfailing support and endless patience. I would also like to thank the late Claire Eastwood an extraordinary teacher and human being who first introduced me to the prophets of the exile.

I'm grateful to my siblings and mother for cheering me on when I was flagging and to my dearest Frank who kindly refrained from offering me any advice but gave me huge amounts of his time, technical ability and encouragement. God bless you all.